Cambridge Elements ≡

Elements in Austrian Economics
edited by
Peter Boettke
George Mason University

THE SOCIALIST CALCULATION DEBATE

Theory, History, and Contemporary Relevance

Peter Boettke
George Mason University

Rosolino A. Candela
Mercatus Center at George Mason University
Universidad Francisco Marroquín

Tegan L. Truitt
George Mason University

CAMBRIDGE
UNIVERSITY PRESS

Shaftesbury Road, Cambridge CB2 8EA, United Kingdom

One Liberty Plaza, 20th Floor, New York, NY 10006, USA

477 Williamstown Road, Port Melbourne, VIC 3207, Australia

314–321, 3rd Floor, Plot 3, Splendor Forum, Jasola District Centre,
New Delhi – 110025, India

103 Penang Road, #05–06/07, Visioncrest Commercial, Singapore 238467

Cambridge University Press is part of Cambridge University Press & Assessment,
a department of the University of Cambridge.

We share the University's mission to contribute to society through the pursuit of
education, learning and research at the highest international levels of excellence.

www.cambridge.org
Information on this title: www.cambridge.org/9781009593663

DOI: 10.1017/9781009593649

When citing this work, please include a reference to the DOI 10.1017/9781009593649

First published 2024

A catalogue record for this publication is available from the British Library

ISBN 978-1-009-59366-3 Hardback
ISBN 978-1-009-59363-2 Paperback
ISSN 2399-651X (online)
ISSN 2514-3867 (print)

The Socialist Calculation Debate

Theory, History, and Contemporary Relevance

Elements in Austrian Economics

DOI: 10.1017/9781009593649
First published online: December 2024

Peter Boettke
George Mason University

Rosolino A. Candela
Mercatus Center at George Mason University
Universidad Francisco Marroquín

Tegan L. Truitt
George Mason University

Author for correspondence: Peter Boettke, peter.boettke@gmail.com

Abstract: For over a generation, the collapse of communism in the Soviet Union and Eastern and Central Europe delegitimized the abolition of private property in the means of production and the practice of central planning as an effective way to achieve the ends of socialism. However, the aspiration of achieving the ends of socialism remains to this day. This Element provides a narrative of a century-long debate that was initiated by Ludwig von Mises in 1920. In so doing, it tells the history of the problem of economic calculation in the socialist commonwealth and its continuing relevance for developments in economics, political economy, and social philosophy.

Keywords: Mises, Hayek, socialism, calculation, planning

ISBNs: 9781009593663 (HB), 9781009593632 (PB), 9781009593649 (OC)
ISSNs: 2399-651X (online), 2514-3867 (print)

Contents

1 Introduction

1.1 Socialism's Contemporary Relevance

In the September 10, 1990 edition of *The New Yorker*, Robert Heilbroner, the Norman Thomas Professor at the New School for Social Research, summarily announced, "It turns out, of course, that Mises was right. The Soviet system has long been dogged by a method of pricing that produced grotesque misallocations of effort" (1990, p. 92). This was a shocking admission by one of the leading socialist intellectuals in America at the time. However, the evidence of the economic deprivation and political tyranny of the communist regimes in Eastern and Central Europe, as well as the Soviet Union, was by 1990 too obvious to be ignored. This represented a seismic shift in the intellectual landscape concerning the prospect and promise of a socialist economic system. As Heilbroner (1990, p. 91) had first explained in the article:

> In the nineteen-thirties, when I was studying economics, a few economists had already expressed doubts about the feasibility of centrally planned socialism. One of them was Ludwig von Mises, an Austrian of extremely conservative views, who had written of the "impossibility" of socialism, arguing that no Central Planning Board could ever gather the enormous amount of information needed to create a workable economic system. That did not seem a particularly cogent reason to reject socialism, given the irrationalism and incoherence of capitalism during the Great Depression. Our skepticism was fortified when Oscar Lange, a brilliant young Polish economist (who would become the first postwar Polish Ambassador to the United States), wrote two dazzling articles showing that a Board would not need all the information that Mises said it couldn't collect. All that such a Board would have to do, Lange wrote, was watch the levels of inventories in its warehouses: if inventories rose, the obvious thing to do was to lower prices, so that the goods would move out more rapidly; and if inventories were too rapidly depleted, to raise prices in order to discourage sales. Fifty years ago, it was felt that Lange had decisively won the argument for socialist planning.

This new consensus of doubt surrounding the feasibility of socialism was forged by numerous reconsiderations of the famous socialist calculation debate, most thoroughly summarized in Don Lavoie's *Rivalry and Central Planning: The Socialist Calculation Debate Reconsidered* (1985a). For a time it appeared that Lavoie's central message concerning the Austrian critique and the role that monetary calculation plays in the operation of the market process, and how its absence introduces intractable coordination failures was the professional consensus.

However, the transition from socialism to a market economy proved more difficult in practice than what many thought it would be in theory. Moreover, the rise of new problematic issues (real or imagined) associated with globalization, the economic development gap, environmental degradation and climate change, and especially the Global Financial Crisis of 2008, resulted in the tide of opinion shifting once more away from a focus on the administrative dysfunctions of government to the disruptiveness of the reality of political capitalism. Many literatures describe capitalism as a social system of production that is built on the exploitation of the least advantaged, rewards the privileged few, and suffers both from an inherited tendency toward monopoly power and periodic industrial fluctuations that disrupt economies and destroy communities. This general sentiment, combined with technological innovations in computational power, as well as refinements in economic theory associated with mechanism design theory, has led many intellectuals (including economists) once more to begin to question whether the critique of socialist planning offered by Mises was as powerful as the reassessment pressed. Socialism is once more viewed as an antidote to a world in crisis due to capitalism (see Piketty 2021).

Since 2010, several scholarly articles have been published challenging Lavoie's account (1985a) of the socialist calculation debate, in essence recanting Heilbronner's admission. Duncan Foley, for example, another famous professor from the New School of Social Research like Heilbronner, published a pair of articles in 2020 revisiting the historical context and theoretical developments that serve as the background for the debate and concludes that the socialist calculation debate missed the mark. "The real import of the historical choice between socialism and capitalism," Foley (2020a, p. 309) insists, "is precisely what is left out of the socialist calculation debate: the social relations through which people organize themselves to produce."

Before he reaches that conclusion, Foley recounts the debate from his perspective. He summarizes Mises's argument as stating that economic rationality required market-clearing prices for millions of specific goods and services and such a determination of equilibrium prices is beyond the capacity of any central planning mechanism. Foley frames the entire debate in terms of neoclassical welfare economics and general competitive equilibrium theory, which, as we will see, is the *opposite* of how Lavoie insisted we must judge the arguments made by Mises and Hayek. Moreover, Foley also finds Mises's argument primitive precisely because an "irony of history is that at the same time Mises was formulating this argument, Alan Turing and others were laying the theoretical groundwork for the creation of electronic computers which could practically tackle problems of this magnitude" (Foley 2020a, p. 308).

In his follow-up essay, Foley (2020b) stresses the intellectual developments "from Vienna to Santa Fe" by engaging both the technical developments in economic theory and the new techniques of calibration and computation that make possible a more sophisticated treatment of the issues involved in creatively constructing a socialist future. By Vienna, he does not mean the Austrian School of Economics associated with Mises and Hayek, but the mathematical group in Vienna that coalesced around Karl Menger, and included Abraham Wald, John von Neumann, and Oskar Morgenstern. The work of this group, Foley argues, provided the foundation for the radical transformation of economics in the post-WWII era into a mathematical science. The implication of that transformation was that the central problem of the allocation of scarce resources among alternative uses would be subsumed under the banner of optimal control theory. "The power of these mathematical methods and the prestige of mathematics in the natural sciences," Foley states, "disposed many sophisticated thinkers to accept the eventual triumph of optimal control methods as inescapable" (Foley 2020b, p. 314).

Top-down technocratic approaches to economic administration followed. And economists made several innovations in their theoretical models and the technologies of calibration and computing that were to be used by economic managers. To give two examples, consider the input-output models of Wassily Leontief, and the linear programming models of Leonid Kantorovich. Both Leontief and Kantorovich would go on to win the Nobel Prize in economics sciences in 1973 and 1975, respectively, for their theoretical innovations. But Foley points to an interesting twist in the narrative: the cousin of the mathematics of optimal control theory is the mathematics of thermodynamics. This later development meant that the complex nature of the system must be recognized rather than brushed aside for tractability. With these new tools and techniques, Foley (2020b, 322) imagines that "a deep transformation of social relations of production would lead to parallel deep transformations in behavior and feelings of human beings." The exploitation, as well as alienation, of the capitalist system will be relegated to the past through the creative constructive of socialism. It is obvious that now, in reading Foley, as well as a more recent article by Lopez (2021) that whatever consensus might have been achieved at the time of Heilbronner's famous admission that Mises was right has simply faded into memory.

The socialist vision is thus still an animating one for many intellectuals, worthy of our philosophical, scientific, and practical attention. The intellectual challenges to neoliberalism by historians of capitalism, the difficulties witnessed in the transition experience in the former socialist countries, and the apparent success of China have opened a new historical phase of discussion: one that enables "radical economists" to revise the interpretation of the debate once more. The Austrian critique offered by Mises and Hayek, in this revisionist rendering, was not grounded in economic theory, but was merely a cover for their political ideology and normative commitments, and thus should have no claim to an objective assessment of the operation of economic systems. To Lopez, the theoretical grounds for assessment are standard neoclassical welfare economics, and socialist planning is just another tool in the economist's tool kit, alongside more conventional interventionist policies, to combat the inefficiencies, instability, and inequities of the market economy. However, one of the frustrating realities in these discussions is that there are so many sources of confusion that the debate easily goes off in directions where no meeting of minds is possible. This Element attempts to reorient the terms of the discussion squarely within the domain of economics and political economy. In doing so, we hope to uncover common ground upon which arguments can be adjudicated. This is admittedly tricky in discussions where the subtext is obviously charged with normative presumptions as well as aesthetic judgments of both the actual world and possible futures.

Lavoie (1985a) stressed that Mises, Hayek, Robbins, Lange, and Lerner were talking past each other, rather than engaging each other's arguments. What is to be learned in this confusion is a major theme of Lavoie's book and also our account to follow. As Israel Kirzner (1988) has stressed, it is in the context of the socialist calculation debate of the 1930s and 1940s that the Austrian economists came to realize the unique and defining characteristics of their approach to the study of economic systems, as well as the theoretical examination of market theory and the price system in particular.

Our Element will attempt to provide an overview of more than a century of professional dialogue about the significance of Mises's economic calculation argument and its implications for economics and political economy. Our goal is to be as thorough and as clear in presenting the argument and its implications as we can be, and to persuade the reader of the centrality of economic calculation for any and all social systems of exchange, production, and distribution. The achievement of a "Good Society" is simply not possible without the ability to engage in rational economic calculation.

In popular, as well as academic presentation, socialism aspires to guarantee every man, woman, and child in the society with basic economic rights, such that they have universal access to high-quality health care, free education, a guaranteed job, affordable housing, a secure retirement, and a clean environment. Such a policy program summarizes socialism as an *aspiration*. In more poetic presentations, socialism does not just tame, but eradicates, the evils of capitalism. While modern socialist aspirations are not immediately associated with a strong view of the means for the achievement of these goals, there remains a promise of more government control and more government redistribution, though guided by the democratic process.

The repeated emphasis on *democratic* socialism in popular and academic discussions was designed to address the social ills of want, ignorance, disease, squalor, and idleness. While socialist rhetoric inclined strongly against bourgeois democracy, it endorsed what at the time they described as *real* democracy. In short, the socialists demanded power for the working people, against the vested interests of the capitalist class. However, the emphasis on *democratic socialism* is not new, as we will see especially in discussing the British market socialists of the 1930s. The tragedy of the twentieth century is that the pursuit of high ideals via the means of socialist planning ended in a totalitarian nightmare. The modifier "democratic" is supposed to correct for all earlier indictments of central planning and totalitarian experiences of the twentieth century.

The key to understanding this tragic experience can be found in the economic analysis of socialism. The *economic analysis* of socialism, which we will continually stress throughout this Element, is focused on the effectiveness of the chosen means to the achievement of those given ends. We will not debate the desirableness of the aspiration, only the efficacy of the means to the attainment of those ends. Ironically, the aspirations and rhetoric of socialists from the last century upon careful examination were not all that different from today.

1.2 Mises's *Socialism* and the Socialist Calculation Debate

The socialist calculation debate was not merely a theoretical controversy. Although socialism arose out of popular appeal, this theoretical debate was inspired by practical attempts to implement socialism in the aftermath of World War I, particularly in Soviet Russia. It was in this historical context that Ludwig von Mises (1881–1973) published his book *Gemeinwirtschaft*, later translated *Socialism: An Economic and Sociological Analysis* ([1922] 1981). This work followed on and augmented an earlier (1920) article, "Die Wirtschaftsrechnung im sozialistischen Gemeinwesen" (*Economic Calculation in the Socialist Commonwealth*), which began as a reply to the recent work of Otto Neurath on the "natural economy" and the promise of socialism. Mises's article immediately generated a heated exchange of ideas in the German language journals and periodicals of the time, invoking responses by Jacob Marschak and Karl Polanyi. It also generated responses in the English language literature already in the 1920s by Fred Taylor and Frank Knight. Mises's *Gemeinwirthschaft* would have a major impact on both F. A. Hayek (and his contemporaries in Austria) and Lionel Robbins (and his contemporaries in England). Mises's 1920 article would only be translated and published in English for the first time in 1935 in a volume edited by Hayek, entitled *Collectivist Economic Planning*. And, since the mid 1920s, Robbins was working with Mises to get his book translated and published in English (this was finally accomplished in 1936). The challenge Mises put forth concerning socialism and systems of social cooperation would stimulate research over the next 100 years in a variety of directions.

1.3 Hodgson's Recent Challenge

Recently Geoffrey Hodgson has returned to this debate, given the renewed interest in socialist ideas among students and members of the cultural and political elite. In *Is Socialism Feasible?* (2019), Hodgson tackles both what he calls "Big Socialism" and "Small Socialism" and the implications of the argument for the varieties of capitalism discussion and the future alternatives for a humane and just political economy. However, in *Wrong Turnings: How the Left Got Lost* (2018), Hodgson provides a warning of how that quest for a humane and just political economy can be derailed due to populism and loose thinking about the organization of society, and a mix of innocence of what economic reasoning can provide and opportunism by strategic but bad faith actors. To counter the wrong turns, Hodgson argues that the Left must embrace its roots in the Enlightenment values of liberty, equality, and universal rights. In short, the answer to the wrong turns provides the path toward a more humane and just future. But to get on that path, one must first understand in detail why the traditional socialist path does not provide that answer.

Hodgson does not endorse the laissez-faire path that Mises and Hayek suggested either. Despite the limits of knowledge and the complexity of the economic system that make socialist economic planning infeasible, Hodgson argues that there remains a critical role of the state and targeted interventions in creating a society based on liberal solidarity. "A better defense of markets and private property," he writes, "would know better their limitations" (Hodgson 2018, p. 190). A market society is embedded, Hodgson argues, in a web of social relationships that "build trust and transcend the monetary calculus of cost and reward." We must move beyond the myth of the universal market, and instead understand the broader social infrastructure that makes commercial society work for all rather than the privileged few. Yet, at the same time, while he deeply shares the concerns of the Left over the "extreme inequalities of income and wealth; poverty and destitution; low wages; appalling working conditions; the lack of access to good education; inadequate healthcare provision; discrimination by race, gender, sexuality or beliefs; the ravaging of the planet by uncaring corporations or governments; the threat of climate change;

and illegal and unjustified wars" (Hodgson 2018, p. 192), he is concerned that they are not approaching the achievement of these goals with the appropriate analytical mindset.

Hodgson's expressed concern is that those on the Left do not pay enough attention to the politico-economic conditions that are necessary to sustain human rights and democracy. Correcting that fundamental flaw would require that we recognize that "the theoretical critique of collectivist socialist planning by von Mises and Hayek is one of the most important intellectual achievements of the twentieth century" (Hodgson 2018, p. 183). Failure to appreciate their argument, Hodgson warns, ultimately leads one to be blind to the "fundamental problems" that public ownership and central planning face in organizing an economic system (Hodgson 2019, p. 72). Socialist planning suffers, despite the best of intentions, from incentive and information issues that results in "bureaucratic ossification and political despotism" and lack of "innovation and economic growth" as well as "curtailed democracy and diminished freedom of expression" (Hodgson 2019, p. 73). Neither laissez-faire liberalism nor central planning socialism offers us a picture of a humane and just future. Instead, the picture Hodgson is painting for the future humane and just political economy is one that accepts the Mises–Hayek critique but embraces the normative concerns often identified with the Left. He has further elaborated this argument in his book *Liberal Solidary: The Political Economy of Social Democratic Liberalism* (2021).

Despite the narrative that has been constructed, mostly by hostile critics, the argument that Hodgson has developed is not that far off from the one Mises, Hayek, and Robbins sought to articulate in the first half of the twentieth century to counter the rising threats from fascist Germany and communist Russia. Their ideas were utilized in Walter Lippmann's *The Good* Society (1937) in a strikingly similar way to how Hodgson leverages them in the current discussion. One must never forget that Mises, Hayek, and Robbins consistently opposed all systems of privilege and fought throughout their respective careers against odious racial and nationalistic doctrines. They were free traders and believers in the free movement of capital and people throughout the globe. Mises ([1927] 2005), for example, declared himself in the 1920s as a cosmopolitan liberal, and maintained that position till his death in 1973. This Element is not the place to settle the interpretative score on the politics of Mises and Hayek, simply because, before that can be addressed, one must clarify precisely the *positive economics* of their argument against socialist economic planning and its implications for the *methodology* and *analytics* of economics before we contemplate the broader range *social philosophical* implications.

1.4 Roadmap

Section 2 articulates the original debate. We present Marxian socialism, and its other nineteenth century variants, as economists in the early twentieth century would have understood them. Socialism in this sense specifies not only aspirations but also the means of achieving the stated ends. We then discuss Mises's initial response to Otto Neurath, as recorded in his 1920 article and more importantly in his 1922 book, *Socialism*. Mises's argument, in short, runs as follows:

1. Without private property in the means of production, there can be no market for the means of production.
2. Without a market for the means of production, there can be no exchange ratios established, and relative prices will not reflect the scarcity of the different goods and services that constitute the means of production.
3. Without prices reflecting relative scarcities, there will be no way for economic decision-makers to engage in rational economic calculation.

The problem with socialism, for Mises, is an *epistemic* one. Prices give producers knowledge that emerges from a rivalrous, competitive process. Without such prices, producers will not know how to allocate scarce resources toward their highest-valued consumer ends, rendering rational economic calculation impossible. Therefore, without the ability to engage in rational economic calculation, there will be no rational way to sort from the array of technologically feasible production projects those that are economically viable. The result is systemic waste, a distorted capital structure, and endemic coordination failures in a socialist economic system. In short, the inability to engage in rational economic calculation means that the socialist means (collective ownership over the means of production) will be incoherent with the achievement of socialist ends (rationalization of production resulting in a burst of productivity).

In Section 3, we discuss the response of the market socialists. Oskar Lange and Abba Lerner develop a theory of market socialism to overcome the calculation problem as described by Mises. They argued that production could be made more efficient *via* socialization, provided that a market for consumer goods remained. In other words, consumers could tell the central planning board what and how much to produce by spending their money, just as in a market economy. But the planning board, with access to better technical knowledge, will be able to produce what consumers want more efficiently. Mises and Hayek develop their responses to this argument by pointing out that there remains a calculation problem in producer-goods markets. There are many technically feasible ways to produce something, only a subset of which are economically feasible. Prices are required to communicate the relative scarcities of steel and platinum so that we keep from building railroad tracks out of platinum rather than steel, even if it is a technologically superior metal.

In Section 4, we discuss the end of the debate in twentieth century. Between the writings of Don Lavoie (1985a, 1985b) and the fall of communism in 1989, economists came to a consensus that the Mises–Hayek criticism of socialist planning was correct. Socialism – the abolition of private property in the means of production – was incapable of outperforming the competitive market economy in theory, and the capitalist system with respect to economic growth and development in practice. Instead, the socialist reality was plagued with pervasive shortages, dysfunctional state enterprises, coordination failures that resulted in grotesque misallocations of labor and capital, and consumer frustration in obtaining not only durable goods but everyday goods and services.

Section 5 turns to new additions to the debate since the collapse of communism. Cockshott (1990) and more recently King and Petty (2021) have argued that socialism of the old variety (what Hodgson dubbed "Big Socialism") – complete nationalization of the means of production – is no longer irrational due to advances in computing technology. The calculation problem has been overcome by the advent of artificial intelligence, which can amalgamate knowledge of relative scarcities better than the price system. Other claims for socialism are more modest: people frequently tend to think that private property should not be entirely abolished, but instead curtailed in particular industries where social injustice is perpetuated, such as housing and healthcare (Durbin 1985). In these literatures, particular emphasis is placed on the modifier "democratic." Democratic control of socialist policy is intended to prevent the excesses of communist dictatorship witnessed in the twentieth century. We argue that there are critical features of the calculation argument missed by contemporary socialists that will serve to undermine the agenda and produce instead unintended and undesirable consequences. Despite the rise of AI and the humbler aims of the contemporary progressive Left, the calculation problem remains present in an insoluble form. Finally, in Section 6, we discuss ways in which the calculation debate has inspired and intersected with other subfields in modern economics.

2 The Original Debate: From Marx to Mises

2.1 Socialism in Classical Economics

One of the oldest arguments in intellectual history is Aristotle's critique of communal property ownership in Plato's *Republic*. Aristotle's argument is a straightforward incentive argument: when everyone owns everything, nobody has any incentive to care about the judicious and efficacious use of that resource, and they will all soon find that resource poorly managed and ultimately depleted. But that argument did not deter the moralistic critique of private property ownership, let alone the commercial activities and profit-seeking behavior from being roundly criticized by the Crown, the Altar, and eventually the secular intelligentsia. Deirdre McCloskey (2006) in the first of her Bourgeois Era trilogy refers to "the clerisy" ever since 1848 as being decidedly critical of the private property and commercial society.[1] McCloskey's effort in large part could be understood as a persistent and consistent effort to update and defend the *doux commerce thesis* that one reads in Montesquieu, Voltaire, Hume, and Smith. But one must remember that this thesis was challenged by Rousseau and eventually by Marx. Rather than a source of a "softening" of our nature, private property and commerce hardened us through alienation and exploitation. As the young Marx argued in his *Economic and Philosophical Manuscripts of 1844* ([1932] 1988) private property was the alienating ability of mankind.

Among the many critics of nineteenth century commercial society, Marx argued that the systematic tendency of industrial societies toward monopoly and periodic economic crises had deeper roots that must be addressed than what mere reform measures could get at. The capitalist system suffered from the fundamental problems of alienation and exploitation. Furthermore, Marx argued that since alienation was rooted to the existence of private property rights, the only way to eradicate the exploitation endemic to capitalism was through a transcendence of the alienating ability of private property. Marx's revolutionary project entailed the abolition of private property in the means of production. In a somewhat colorful analogy, Marx tackled the age-old proverb that "money is the root of all evil" by suggesting to his comrades that trying to eradicate the evils of capitalism by abolishing money would be similar to trying to get rid of the evils of the Catholic Church by abolishing the Pope. It doesn't work. But, if we could abolish Catholicism, then there would be no need for a Pope. Similarly, if we abolish the private property capitalist economy, there would be no need for money and profit-seeking.

The promise that Marx held out for his system was that once the alienating and exploitative system of capitalism was transcended, the new system could *rationalize* production, and result in a corresponding burst of productivity which would deliver mankind from the "Kingdom of Necessity" to the "Kingdom of Freedom." The burst of productivity would lift us from the burdens of scarcity and trade-offs, and deliver us instead into a world that

---

[1] For McCloskey "the clerisy" is synonymous with the intelligentsia or intellectual class in society.

would overcome the rigid reality of the division of labor. As Marx (and Engels) argued in *The German Ideology* ([1846] 1939) we would no longer have to be a hunter, a herder, a fisherman, or a laborer, but instead could be all of those without the need to specialize. The central puzzle of society would no longer be what institutions enable us to realize productive specialization and peaceful cooperation among diverse, distant, and often divergent individuals, but instead how the rationalization of production will result in the end of class conflict and harmony among peoples.

This promise of a utopia of total freedom grew in inspiration as the era of nineteenth century industrialization spread throughout Europe. This era was not without its amazing signs of progress. As Karl Marx and Friedrich Engels write in *The Communist Manifesto* ([1848] 1998), the bourgeoise had delivered for mankind an increase in the standard of living that was unprecedented in human history. Marx and Engels were not nineteenth century versions of "slow growth" and "small is beautiful" critics of capitalism. To understand the subsequent debate, the critical point to remember is the argument about *rationalizing production* and *burst of productivity*. As Marx and Engels state ([1848] 1998, p. 75), the "proletariat will use its political supremacy to wrest, by degrees, all capital from the bourgeoisie, to centralise all instruments of production in the hands of the state, i.e., of the proletariat organised as the ruling class; and to increase the total of productive forces as rapidly as possible." The waste and destruction that was endemic to the capitalist process of development result from the "invisible hand" of the market, which led to chaotic processes of exchange and production based on the seeking of profits. Moreover, this process was characterized by increasing monopolization of industry, punctuated by periodic economic crises, followed by even more increasing monopolization. This process of monopolistic power exploiting the working class as well as nature represented the natural outcome of this "invisible hand" process going on behind the backs of those impacted. Marx wanted to take the invisible, and make it transparent, and thus subject it to rational control. Thus, the abolition of private property would be followed by a substitution of production for direct use under the direction of the central planner for production for profit and exchange guided by the anarchy of the market. It is important to stress that Marx did not believe that the new system would have a permanent planning bureaucracy, precisely because with the rationalization of production and the corresponding burst of productivity, no permanent division of labor would emerge. We would rotate in and out of the various tasks required by the community of mankind harmoniously. Questions of incentives and opportunistic behavior were not relevant to the new socialist world because a new socialist man would populate that world.

By the late nineteenth century and early twentieth century, the spread of socialist ideas throughout the industrial economies gave moral weight to the critique of capitalism. The excesses of the existing system did appear to result in inequality and injustice, periodic financial turbulence, and unemployment, and the brutality of colonialism and war. Within bourgeois society, various countervailing forces were proposed to tame the forces of capitalism, such as unions, welfare legislation, and the regulation of industry. However, reform measures alone would never be able to adequately address the ills of capitalism. Only a revolutionary transformation of the social system of production would be able to achieve the goals of socialism. With rising political tensions in Europe and the outbreak of World War I, socialist movements throughout Europe and the US moved into the mainstream of discussion. The older Manchester liberalism was no longer an animating force throughout Europe, and laissez-faire liberalism was discredited in the US, replaced by progressivism in thought and politics.

Revolutionary socialism was a live option in Europe and the US during the 1910s and especially immediately after World War I. So were other forms of socialism, such as Fabianism and evolutionary socialism. But the most intellectually consistent and bold version of socialism was that of the Marxist–Leninist revolutionary socialism. There were short-lived revolutions in Germany and elsewhere in the late 1910s, but the Russian Revolution ushered in the world's first explicitly Marxist revolutionary regime. For our subsequent presentation, it is critical to note that one of the experiences with various socialist initiatives was Austria during the period of the "Red Vienna" (1918–1934).

This quick sample of historical background was necessary to set the intellectual context for the subsequent socialist calculation debate. One of the most famous economists in the world at the end of the nineteenth and early twentieth century was Eugen Böhm-Bawerk, who, along with Friedrick Wieser, represented the second generation of the Austrian marginalist-subjectivist school of economic thought following in the footsteps of Carl Menger. Menger was recognized as one of the co-developers of modern neoclassical economic theory. Böhm-Bawerk's book *Capital and Interest* ([1884–1921] 1959) was a leading text throughout the German-speaking world presenting modern neoclassical economic theory, explaining how markets function to coordinate exchange and price factors of production, guided by subjective valuation and cost. Böhm-Bawerk also was the author of *Karl Marx and the Close of His System* ([1896] 1898), which was at its time of publication taken to be the most devastating critique of the Marxist theory of capitalist exploitation. Böhm-Bawerk's works were translated into English, and he was an active participant in the emerging international community of professional economists. His students included, among others, both Joseph Schumpeter and Ludwig Mises. Also in attendance at his graduate seminars were Austro-Marxists Otto Bauer, Rudolf Hilferding, and Otto Neurath, and Russian Marxist and subsequent economic theorist of the Bolshevik Revolution, Nikolai Bukharin.

Neurath would develop an argument along Marxist lines that he thought answered Böhm-Bawerk's challenge and was faithful to the rationalization of production projects based on "the Natural Economy." He would also later join the German Social Democratic Party and ran the office for central economic planning in Munich between 1918 and 1919. Hilferding, author most famously of *Finance Capital* ([1910] 1981), was also the main Marxist theorist who attempted to counter Böhm-Bawerk's arguments about the logical flaws in the Marxist system, and he would emerge as the main theoretician for the German Social Democrats and served as finance minister of Germany in 1923. Bukharin, the main economic architect of Bolshevik policies from 1917 to 1928, also authored a critique of the Austrian economists in a book written before the Russian Revolution entitled *The Economic Theory of the Leisure Class* (1927).[2] Bauer would rise to leadership within the ruling Austrian Social Democrats and would serve as the foreign minister of the Republic of German-Austria in 1918 and 1919. Bauer and Mises were close friends, but Neurath and Mises were not.

As the Social Democrats after World War I rose to positions of political leadership in Vienna, Mises's own research interests shifted from monetary theory and policy, as was reflected in his *The Theory of Money and Credit* ([1912] 1981), to the appropriate domestic and international policies required to recover from the devastation of war, and can be seen in his *Nation, State and Economy* ([1919] 2006). Mises, as many academics in Europe at that time, pursued a scientific career while holding down a day job as an economic advisor to the government at an independent policy advisory entity, which was similar in structure and scope, we would argue, to the National Economic Advisory Council that was established in the 1920s by the Labor government of Ramsey MacDonald, in which Pigou, Keynes, and Robbins all served as members. Mises was responsible for providing economic analysis on proposed governmental initiatives during the waning years of the Habsburg Empire, under the Social Democratic regime during the Red Vienna period, and during the short-lived conservative government of Engelbert Dollfus. Mises worked as a senior economist at the Austrian Chamber of Commerce and Industry from 1909 until he took up his chaired professorship in Geneva in 1934, except for his time in military service during WWI. He also served in several other capacities on

---

[2] The book Bukharin tells us was completed in 1914, it was published in Russian in 1919, and in English in 1927. Boettke (1990) devotes considerable space discussing Bukharin's role in the Bolshevik revolution and the Soviet experience with socialism in that first decade.

behalf of the government of Austria, including heading up an agency responsible for international debt settlements after WWI, and as Austria's representative in various international trade negotiations. From his position as an advisory economist, he wrote many reports on both domestic and international public policy initiatives during the interwar years (see Ebeling 2000, 2002, 2012).

There certainly were plenty of domestic policy initiatives over which Mises had to provide analysis during his twenty-five years at the chamber, such as public housing, health and human services, as well as fiscal and monetary policy. This was especially the case after the Social Democrats rose to controlling power in 1918. His friend Otto Bauer was committed to initiating steps toward the revolutionary transformation of the economy along Marxist lines, while his classmate but not friend Otto Neurath was involved in actively developing arguments for "calculation in kind" and "an economy in kind," where the administrative economy would plan production and consumption. Neurath was also engaged in a public propaganda effort to communicate to the people directly the promissory benefits of the administrative economy. This would lead in the later 1920s to his effort through the *Gesellschafts und Wirtschaftsmuseum* and the isotype (picture language) to spread popular support for total socialization. But in the period immediately following WWI, he was arguing for how the organization of the war economy could be used to jump-start the transition to the "natural economy." It is the transition to an in-kind economy that would lay the foundation for what Neurath described as "total socialization." With the Social Democrats in power, these ideas moved from idle speculation of a theorist who had not learned his lessons in Böhm-Bawerk very well, to actual proposals that had a real possibility of being implemented.

2.2 Mises's *Socialism*

It is in this context that Mises felt compelled to put pen to paper and author his "Economic Calculation in the Socialist Commonwealth" in late 1919, published in 1920, followed by his further elaboration of the critique in *Socialism: An Economic and Sociological Analysis* in 1922. Mises understood he was not the first economist or social thinker to criticize socialism. However, as recognized by Hoff ([1938] 1949, p. 1), the "economist who has done more than any other to bring the problem up for discussion is Professor Ludwig von Mises." So central were Mises's arguments to the problem of economic calculation under socialism that all economic arguments after 1920 were intended to reinforce or respond to Mises's argument (Lavoie 1985a). Despite Mises's already strong priors as a liberal, it is important to stress that he was even more committed, perhaps because of his own strong commitments, to the Weberian strategy of bringing dispassionate *scientific* analysis to heated public policy disputes, and in a way that could produce resolutions between the different parties to the dispute. Moral disputes and condemnations tended to fail to produce any common ground. The business of the social scientist, according to Max Weber's strict value-freedom argument (*wertfreiheit*), is to treat ends as given, and not to question them, limiting one's critical analysis only to assessing the efficacy of the chosen means (policies) to achieve these given ends (improved common welfare). This was positive economics prior to the positivistic philosophy of science, which would emerge during this period from the Vienna Circle. In this vein, it is interesting to note that Weber ([1918] 1967) independently offered an argument strongly resembling Mises's calculation argument.

Mises implemented value-freedom in his analysis consistently and persistently throughout this period. Although a staunch defender of *laissez-faire* economics and classical liberalism, Mises argued that socialism was a bold idea and as such it demanded analytically careful as well as critical scrutiny. He certainly understood the appeal of the socialist doctrine and its aspirations, and he also understood that subjecting that doctrine to critical scrutiny would most likely bring with it harsh condemnation. But he also felt that as a scholar and a man of reason, thrust into the middle of the practical reality of a theory being implemented into public policy, he could stand there and do nothing other than engage in the logical exercise of diagnosing the efficacy of socialist means with respect to achieving the aspirational goals of socialism.

Mises argued that it was not possible for socialist means to achieve the stated goals of socialism. No rationalization of production would be forthcoming; no burst of productivity; no harmony of the class interests. Instead, production would be chaotic, wealth would be destroyed, and the social climate would devolve into a war of all against all as people would struggle for their material survival. Although Mises's argument is well known, we believe his reasons for making such a stark claim are less well understood. If Mises's challenge was not such a strong one both in terms of the nature of the claim and more importantly in the elementary logic of his presentation, then the list of leading economists and the subsequent literature devoted to refuting his argument would simply be unexplainable. In short, Mises provided a counterargument against the possibility of socialism not in terms of its stated ends, but the means by which to achieve its stated ends. "Like all other forms of social organization," Mises states, "Socialism is only a means, not an end in itself" (Mises [1922] 1981, p. 406). "But that Socialism alone has the public welfare in view can at once be denied." A market economy and a socialist economy "differ not in their aims but in the means by which they wish to pursue them" ([1922] 1981, p. 46).

The critical lynchpin in Mises's argument was that the rationalization of production projects would be rendered senseless in the move to total socialization because, without private property in the means of production, there would be no way for economic actors to engage in *rational economic calculation*. And, without the ability to engage in economic calculation, economic actors will have no meaningful way to sort from the array of technologically feasible projects those that are economically viable. Just a quick note – all systems of social cooperation must have some mechanism that enables the system itself to sort from imagined normatively desired states to feasible states, and furthermore from feasible to economically viable. We must move the discourse from imagined futures to possible worlds. Nirvana is not an option for humanity, so in contemporary philosophical parlance, ideal theorizing must be disciplined by social science so we get nonideal theorizing as a guide to the "desirable." Marx was critical of utopian socialists, and so must we be today, as certainly Mises was in his time.

Note that this critique of rational economic calculation is not a moral critique of socialism. But for the sake of argument, Mises was willing to grant the moral case for communal property and the assumption of a new socialist man. And even with granting these assumptions to his intellectual adversaries, Mises believed he was able to demonstrate that socialism was logically incoherent with respect to means-ends analysis. Without the ability to engage in rational economic calculation, there was simply no mechanism by which collective ownership in the means of production could result in a rationalization of production. There would be no way to ensure that the social system of exchange and production was producing more with less, rather than less with more.

2.3 Economic Calculation

To unpack this argument, one must return to first principles about the role of property rights in exchange, the role that exchange ratios (i.e., prices) play in guiding exchange and production decisions, and finally, how the price system and profit-and-loss accounting reinforce one another to cajole, prod, and discipline economic actors. Economic calculation is a tool for the human mind that enables decision-makers to negotiate the myriad of trade-offs amidst the bewildering throng of economic possibilities. Without it, those decision-makers are reduced to making so many stabs in the dark. In short, the opposite of rationalizing production would take place.

Mises returned to first principles precisely because too many socialists "never come to grips in any way with the problems of economics, and who have made no attempt at all to form for themselves any clear conception of the conditions which determine the character of human society" ([1920] 1975, p. 87). They have neglected the fundamental problems of the organization of economic activity, and instead are content with "painting lurid pictures of existing conditions and glowing pictures of that golden age which is the natural consequence of the New Dispensation" ([1920] 1975, p. 88). Despite this frustrating state of discourse, Mises insists that investigating the conditions of the economic organization of socialism is far more than merely an interesting intellectual exercise. It enables us to get at the core principles that explain the conditions that make possible social cooperation under the division of labor.

Socialism, at the time of Mises's writing, had a very specific meaning, and this must always be remembered in assessing the argumentative claims in the subsequent debate. Socialism theoretically and practically meant "all the means of production are the property of the community" (Mises [1920] 1975, p. 89). And the community will deploy its authority over the use, maintenance, and disposal of this property through the establishment of an administrative body tasked with this purpose. This administrative body will be entrusted to make decisions concerning staffing, administrative tasks, and goals all with the explicit purpose of articulating and representing the general will of the community. In the socialist vision, consumption decisions are separated from production decisions. The consumption questions in terms of *who* and *what* is to be consumed is a question of socialist distribution. But the *how* question of production is the critical question for the economic organization of the socialist society. The administrative body will have to determine the use of factors of production to produce the greatest yield and minimize waste in order to meet the goal of rationalizing production.

To Mises, "it lies in the very nature of socialist production that the shares of the particular factors of production in the national dividend cannot be ascertained, and that *it is impossible* in fact to gauge the relationship between expenditure and income" (emphasized added; [1920] 1975, p. 90). For the sake of argument, Mises put aside discussions of how the distribution of consumption goods among the citizens of the future socialist economy would be determined. Whether such dictums like "from each according to their abilities to each according to their need" could be successfully implemented was of secondary importance. He argued that what was of primary importance, no matter how the problem of distribution was supposedly addressed, was the "productivity of social labor." Comrades can eat several times a day, find adequate shelter, have clothes on their backs, and experience occasional amusement only if the problems of production under socialism could be solved. Thus, if Mises's argument could demonstrate that production in a world of communal property rights would result not in a rationalization of production, but in planned chaos, then the force of his argument would indeed be strong and would have to be reckoned with for any serious proposal for socialism to be operational.

Without the institutional infrastructure of the free enterprise economy, namely private property in the means of production, there would be no market for means of production, and thus no monetary prices established on that market. Without these monetary prices – which serve as aids to the human mind – economic decision-makers will be unable to form calculated judgments about alternative courses of action and engage in judicious assessment of past decisions and appraisement of possibly more productive future paths. The commercial society is predicated on private property rights to provide incentives to decision-makers to husband resources efficiently, for relative prices to guide them in their efforts, for profits to lure them, and for losses to discipline them. Absent private property rights, decision-makers are left without prices, and without prices, profit-and-loss statements are rendered economically meaningless. As would later be stressed in subsequent rounds of the debate, prices without property are a grand illusion (Nutter 1968).

2.4 Alternative Methods of Accounting

Much of Mises's original 1920 article is devoted to demonstrating not only this foundational point, but also arguing that various efforts to engage in calculation-in-kind, whether through labor coupons or some other scheme, do not provide an adequate substitute for monetary prices and profit-and-loss accounting. In the case of labor time associated with production serving as the basis for economic calculation, the impracticality of this solution is revealed as soon as it is recognized that labor is not uniform and homogeneous. There are qualitative differences between the types of labor as well as the laborers themselves that result in different valuations and thus supply and demand configurations for labor. Without relative prices established on the market, and monetary calculation of alternative courses of productive activity, there is once again no obvious way to connect the different types of labor to the process of production.

In a competitive economy, the higgling and bargaining on the market to use Adam Smith's phraseology, produces a set of exchange ratios. These exchange ratios reflect the subjective assessment of trade-offs that economic actors make in the course of their choices on the market, their buying and abstaining from buying, and their offering for sale or withdrawal from sale. This process of competing bids and asks results in an array of prices for goods of the lower order (consumption) and higher order (factors of production). The subjective assessments of trade-offs by some become the "objective" data of the market for others, as they weigh their subjective trade-offs. The process in its entirety both generates and communicates the relevant knowledge to others so they may formulate their production plans and expectations about consumer demand for the goods and services they are offering to the market. Critical to understanding the capitalist process of exchange and production is that it is a voyage into the unknown future, "and that its *economic* consequence remains uncertain even if it is *technically* successful. They see in the uncertainty which leads to specula- tion a consequence of the anarchy of production, whilst in fact it is a necessary result of changing economic conditions" (emphasis original; Mises [1922] 1981, p. 188). As such, there is a need for an economic compass to guide those embarking on the voyage. To Mises, that compass is the price system.

The market price system has three advantages that are critical for exchange, production, and thus distribution. First, the array of relative prices that exist at the time of decision-making provides the necessary *ex ante* knowledge for estimating expenditures relative to potential receipts. Economic actors want to buy low and sell high, so they study prices prior to making a decision about alternative courses of action. Second, the price system, and in particular profit- and-loss accounting, provides decision-makers with *ex post* knowledge about the appropriateness or inappropriateness of their previous courses of action. If they bought low, but could sell high, the market process reveals the essential correctness of their decision to them in the form of profits, while if they bought high, but can only sell low, the market process disciplines them for their bad decision through the penalty of loss. But the guiding and revealing functions of the market system do not exhaust its advantageous characteristics for coordin- ating exchange and production decisions among a multitude of participants. Third, the process of juxtaposing the *ex ante* expectations with the *ex post* realizations sets in motion the *discovery* by economic actors of better ways to pursue their course of action. The market, in this sense, is constantly discover- ing errors and leading to their correction through the adjustments and adapta- tions of economic decision-makers. The market process is constantly adapting and readapting to the ever-changing circumstances of economic life. The important point to stress is that absent the institutional infrastructure of private property, this market process will not be able to operate to provide these three- fold advantages we have just laid out, which ultimately drives the market systems' ability to achieve the complex coordination of economic activity associated with wealth creation and economic progress. An implication of this is that anytime we step outside of the realm of the market economy and monetary calculation, the social system must attempt to provide a substitute for property, prices, and profit-and-loss to align incentives, guide decisions, lure entrants and innovation, and discipline and select superior methods of produc- tion to reveal opportunities for mutually beneficial cooperation. Whether or not these substitutes can effectively serve the function that the price system does is the crux of the debate in comparative institutional analysis.

The fact that the market system and monetary calculation is never perfect, nor that it is not applicable to all questions of social life from the sacred to the profane does not provide a reason to dismiss the significance of the market process for peaceful social cooperation. The point here is that, given that Marx had regarded commodity production for exchange and profit as wasteful, and therefore such waste could be eliminated by abolishing private property, Mises reasserted the necessity of private property as the institutional prerequisite for the detection of waste in the form of entrepreneurial losses, which are revealed in the process of exchange. Eliminating private property in the means of production is analogous to severing a telephone cord between economic decision-makers attempting to communicate with one another the urgency of demands and the least cost methods of production.

For the purposes of everyday economic life, Mises tells his readers, monetary calculation provides all that can be reasonably expected of it. Monetary economic calculation "affords us a guide through the oppressive plenitude of economic potentialities. It enables us to extend to all goods of a higher order the judgment of value, which is bound up with and clearly evident in, the case of goods ready for consumption, or at best of production goods of the lowest order. It renders their value capable of computation and thereby gives us the primary basis for all economic operations with goods of the higher order. Without it, all production involving processes stretching well back in time and all the longest roundabout processes of capitalist production would be groping in the dark" ([1920] 1975, p. 101).

2.5 Coordinating the Division of Labor in Classical Economics

In making this argument, Mises did not think he was necessarily the first to ever stress this point. He did think that his statement refined earlier statements and made them sharper than had previously been stated. But for our purposes, it might make sense to point to similar arguments made among classical economists and the early neoclassical economists prior to returning to Mises's exposition. First, Adam Smith discusses the situation with the coordination of the division of labor in the first chapters of *The Wealth of Nations*. In Book I, in illustrating the complex set of exchange relationships that are required to produce even the most ordinary of goods – a common woolen coat on the back of the day laborer – Smith states clearly that "the number of people whose industry a part, though but a small part, has been employed in procuring him this accommodation, *exceeds all computation*" ([1776] 1976, p. 15, emphasis added). In the very next chapter, we are informed that we cannot rely on benevolence to secure the goods and services required for our daily survival, but must offer favorable terms of trade with our fellow human beings. And, to emphasize the point, Smith states: "In civilized society he stands at all times in need of the cooperation and assistance of great multitudes, while his whole life is scarce sufficient to gain the friendship of a few persons" ([1776] 1976, p. 18). We must, Smith states, appeal to the self-love of our trading partners to secure what we demand from the butcher, the baker, and the brewer. Commercial society based on private property and freedom of exchange enables individuals to pursue productive specialization and realize peaceful social cooperation.

But Smith isn't over here. In Book IV, he explains that efforts to thwart this "invisible hand" process of social cooperation under the division of labor will produce both economic discoordination and the abuse of political power. "What is the species of domestic industry which his capital can employ, and of which the produce is likely to be of the greatest value, every individual, it is evident, can, in his local situation, judge much better than any statesman or lawgiver can do for him." And, he then warns, "The statesman, who should attempt to direct private people in what manner they ought to employ their capitals, would not only load himself with a most unnecessary attention, but assume an authority which could safely be trusted, not only to no single person, but to no council or senate whatever, and which would nowhere be so dangerous as in the hands of a man who had folly and presumption enough to fancy himself fit to exercise it." ([1776] 1976, p. 478)

J. B. Say's *Treatise* ([1803] 1964, pp. 83–84) placed the cultivator, the manufacturer, and the trader at the center of his exposition of commercial life. It is their business to turn a profit through their superior knowledge of market conditions and apply it to achieve the satisfaction of human wants. They achieve this through experimentation. The commercial "adventurer" has their conjectures tested through trade and competition. This hazardous endeavor, Say reports, is on safer grounds when actors can engage in economic calculation. The commercial adventurer is rewarded appropriately if their deployment of capital meets the demands of the consumer. It is this ability to rely on the calculation of alternative uses of capital that turns a potentially hazardous adventure for the merchant into the ordinary business of regular trade and guides them through the necessary adaptations and adjustments necessitated by changing conditions. The market system – its institutions that make it possible such as property, contract, and consent and which give rise to the price system – provides the economic compass to our adventurer. Though Say does not say this explicitly, the implication would be that absent those institutions, the economic compass is not available for the adventurer to rely on in making critical decisions.

J. S. Mill in his *Principles of Political Economy* ([1848] 1965, pp. 140–141, 412–415) would highlight in his presentation of the market system the role of profit and the rate of return on alternative opportunities (in investment, in production, and in occupation). The adjustments and adaptations are not immediate, in fact, they are sometimes gradual and onerous. But not as slow and difficult as is often depicted. Commercial life adapts and evolves, new capital is attracted to where the returns are most favorable, and occupations of higher return attract the attention of the capable. Basically, creative and alert individuals are reading the signals of the market, and weighing the alternative course of action, and again the institutions of property, contract, and consent provide the background against which the market system prods, guides, and selects.

One of the most important points to get across for our narrative is that, as Lionel Robbins stressed in his *The Theory of Economic Policy in the English Classical Political Economists* (1952), the thinkers from Adam Smith to J. S. Mill developed their theory of the liberal market economy side by side with the emerging understanding the liberal political and legal order. The focus on commercial activity was never taken to be in an institutional vacuum, but also against this given background of a liberal political and legal order. Hume's three principles of stability of possession (property), transference of possessions by consent (consent), and the keeping of promises (contract) were never far from the classical economist's mind.

Where Mises expanded upon the classical economists was to illustrate how the division of labor is predicated on a division of knowledge that needs to be coordinated between producers and consumers. But, both the division of labor *and* the division of knowledge are predicated on a *division of ownership*. Thus, for Mises "the social function of private ownership in the means of production" is fundamentally *epistemic*, rather than motivational in nature, since its role "is to put the goods into the hands of those *who know best how to use them*" (emphasis added; Mises [1922] 1981, p. 277). In this way, in "societies based on the division of labour," the exchange of private property in the means of production "effects a kind of *mental division of labour*, without which neither economy nor systematic production would be possible" (emphasis added; [1922] 1981, p. 101).

2.6 Liberalism and Socialism

The challenge of socialism comes into sharp relief once we stress the background of liberal political and legal institutions. Socialism promised to eliminate the social ills of the market by means of the abolition of the political and legal institutions of liberalism. This was the aspiration, until it wasn't. To get a clearer understanding of the debate initiated in 1920, one must go back to that time and understand the alternative system that was being constructed and the proposals that were being implemented to realize that system in practice. Mises in *Human Action* ([1949] 1966) would identify the foundational difficulty that arose in the manner in which liberals had argued their position. In pushing the idea of the common good, "the liberal philosophers themselves contributed an essential element to the notion of the godlike state. They substituted in their inquiries the image of an ideal state for the real states of their age. They constructed the vague image of a government whose only objective is to make its citizens happy" ([1949] 1966, p. 690). But, as Mises was quick to point out, "the liberal philosophers deal only with a state which has nothing in common with these governments of corrupt courts and aristocracies. The state, as it appears in their writings, is governed by a perfect superhuman being, a king whose only aim is to promote the welfare of his subjects" ([1949] 1966, p. 690).

Working from this starting point, the classical political economists of the eighteenth and nineteenth century sought to explore if the unencumbered actions of individuals in society would conflict with the goals of the benevolent and omnipotent King. They surprisingly answered, NO. The private property market economy left free to operate would tend to produce the social outcome that the benevolent and omnipotent King would desire for his society. It is true, they argued, that market participants are selfish and seek their own profit. In the market economy, they argued, entrepreneurs earn profits only by satisfying the demands of the consumers in the most effective manner possible. Thus, in pursuing their own self-interest, the objectives of entrepreneurs ultimately align with those of the perfect king. "For this benevolent king too aims at nothing else than such an employment of the means of production that the maximum of consumer satisfaction can be reached" (Mises [1949] 1966, p. 690).

This way of framing the issue had its pros and cons, and the cons would be on display both by confusing how market society actually works and in the analysis of socialism in theory and practice. The liberals analytically had paved the way, according to Mises, for the socialists, due to this assumption of an all-knowing and all-powerful benevolent state. As he put it, under those assumptions the state must be put in charge of all economic activity:

> This inference became logically inescapable as soon as people began to ascribe to the *state* not only moral but also intellectual perfection. The liberal philosophers had described their imaginary state as an unselfish entity, exclusively committed to the best possible improvement of its subjects' welfare. They had discovered that in the frame of a market society the citizens' selfishness must bring about the same results that this unselfish

state would seek to realize; it was precisely this fact that justified the preservation of the market economy in their eyes. But things became different as soon as people began to ascribe to the *state* not only the best intentions but also omniscience. Then one could not help concluding that the infallible state was in a position to succeed in the conduct of production activities better than erring individuals. It would avoid all those errors that often frustrate the actions of entrepreneurs and capitalists. There would no longer be malinvestment or squandering of scarce factors of production; wealth would multiply. The "anarchy" of production appears wasteful when contrasted with the planning of the *omniscient* state. The socialist mode of production then appears to be the only reasonable system, and the market economy seems the incarnation of unreason. In the eyes of the rationalist advocates of socialism, the market economy is simply an incomprehensible aberration of mankind. (emphasis in original; Mises [1949] 1966, p. 692)

Mises set out to prove that this logical inference was wrong. The state and its decision-makers were not in any position to assume the benevolent and omniscient social planner role in the economic system. Mises would counter the socialist claim. For the sake of argument, Mises would leave the assumption of benevolence intact, but focus the counterargument on the assumption of intellectual perfection. This was consistent with his understanding of the strictures of value-free economic analysis. One of his most subtle arguments is his demonstration that even if socialist central planners are granted the complete information about the *technological possibilities* of their era, they will still not be in possession of the required *economic knowledge* to engage in rational economic calculation (Mises [1920] 1975, p. 120). Without private property rights in the means of production, and thus without a market for the means of production, there would be no way to discover, disseminate, and utilize the context-specific economic knowledge of the relevant trade-offs that must be accounted for in weighing investment and enterprise decisions. There will be no way to sort from the array of technologically feasible projects, those which are economically viable.

2.7 The Progress of the Debate

Between 1920 and 1949, Mises's argument is consistent, but under constant refinement in articulation of the details. Replies from notable scholars poured in, often in agreement, as with Weber ([1921] 2013, also see 1918), but perhaps more often in disagreement, for example, from Karl Polanyi (see Bockman et al. 2016). The *economic* problems socialism would confront were linked to property rights, prices, profit-and-loss, and the institutional infrastructure within which economic, political, and social life takes place. Each stage of his argument relied neither on the maximization of either utility or profits by *homo economicus*, nor the attainment of the optimality conditions of general equilibrium. In short, it is a complete misreading of Mises to see him making anything approximating an argument from within the perfectly competitive market model.

Mises's argument from 1920 to his mature statements in 1949 applies strictly under dynamic conditions of innovation (changing costs of production) as well as evolving tastes (changing demand). Economic calculation presents no problem, according to Mises, under the static conditions of perfect competition and general competitive equilibrium. The Austrian argument, however, has always been that the world in which socialism is possible – a world of zero uncertainty – is not the world in which we live. It's irrelevant to point to the conditions of a general equilibrium and say that, in principle, there is nothing preventing us from solving the system of simultaneous equations that will generate the equilibrium. Of course, there's no issue with solving a system of simultaneous equations, however large the system and tedious the solution may be. The problem is that we are never in a state of general equilibrium because economic life is characterized not by optimality conditions, but by economic actors acting in the face of ignorance and coping with constantly changing conditions. The challenge for socialists is to come up with some sort of alternative means of guiding decisions and providing feedback under conditions of dynamic uncertainty. Despite their best efforts, they still have not done so. To Mises the problems were not static properties, but problems of the processes of adaptation and adjustment to the constantly changing circumstances of human interaction. Optimality conditions, if ever achieved, were a by-product of the analysis of market theory and the price system, *never* an assumption prior to the analysis. Mises was aided in this exercise of refinement most notably by F. A. Hayek.

3 Rebuttals and Refinements: Hayek and the Market Socialists

3.1 F. A. Hayek: Mises's "Student"

When F. A. Hayek moved to Britain in the early 1930s from his native Austria, he was immediately struck by what he saw as the same attitude among British intellectuals as he experienced among German thinkers during the 1920s. In fact, as he wrote to Lionel Robbins 21 July 1931, "I shall certainly look for an opportunity to warn British economists from the fate of Austria and Germany. I am afraid, England too, is already at the beginning of this pernicious road which, once one has progressed far on it, seems to make a return impossible."[3] As Bruce Caldwell (2007, p. 3) highlights, Hayek thought the problem lay with

---

[3] Letter from F.A. Hayek to Lionel Robbins, July 21, 1931, Lionel Robbins Papers, box 130, Early 1930s, LSE Archives and Special Collections; quoted from Caldwell 2020, pp. 721–722.

the fact that the previous generation of economists in their zeal to reject eighteenth and nineteenth century classical political economy had focused their efforts on criticizing the *theoretical* approach to social science, with the consequence of discrediting *economic reasoning* in general.

Hayek's inaugural lecture as the Tooke Chair of Economic Science and Statistics delivered on March 1, 1933 was "The Trend of Economic Thinking" and in that lecture, he made his case for how this loss of economic reasoning resulted in deleterious consequences for economic policy and society at large (Hayek 1933). Hayek argued that economics was born in comparative institutional analysis, including the critical examination of utopian schemes. He also insisted to his readers that liberal economists are no less concerned with the disadvantaged in society than are their intellectual opponents on the Left and that economic theory had vastly improved as a consequence of the marginal revolution and the development of neoclassical theory in the late nineteenth and earlier twentieth century. Ironically, Hayek contended that neoclassical economics had repaired the problems in the classical system identified in the historicist critique, but that the general intellectual world largely ignored these positive developments in the body of economic thought. Instead, the intellectual and policy class proceeded as if the historicist critique held sway over contemporary economic theorizing. As a result, various utopian schemes that would be refuted by careful economic analysis retained popular support which was far in excess of the merits of the schemes. "Refusing to believe in general laws," Hayek argued, "the Historical School had the special attraction that its method was constitutionally unable to refute even the wildest of Utopias, and was, therefore, not likely to bring disappointment associated with theoretical analysis" (1933, p. 125). Bad ideas produce bad policy, and bad policy results in worsening economic conditions for society.

This dismissal of classical political economy by intellectuals meant that once the intellectual discipline that modern economic theory imposed was relaxed, all manner of utopian schemes could be offered to address social ills, from poverty to monopoly power to depression. The necessary scientific and philosophical task of submitting the various proposals for social reform to critical analysis capable of sorting from the postulated desirable to the potentially feasible, and ultimately to the actually viable was simply abandoned by the intelligentsia. This is the consequence of the rejection of the teachings of economics and political economy that the German Historical School accomplished, and which was being replicated in the UK and the US. The value-free analysis of value-laden proposals through strict means-ends examination was rejected. In this assessment, Robbins was also in agreement that a defense of economic theory had to be mounted for the current generation. This project to ground economic policy discourse in sound theory motivated much of the joint ventures of Hayek and Robbins between 1930 and 1950, including not only their own books and articles as well as the translations and reprints they marshaled into publication, but also the visitors and seminar culture they created at the London School of Economics (LSE) (see Boettke and Candela 2020).

3.2 The Threat of Collectivist Planning and *The Road to Serfdom*

To counter the confusion caused by this state of economic education and the general misunderstanding of the events in Germany, Hayek wrote a memo to Lord Beveridge in 1933 (see Caldwell 2007, pp. 245–248), in which he expressed his concern that unless the confusion is cleared up, the countries of Western Europe will go down the same road as Germany to the destruction of civilization as we know it.[4] The British economy, one must remember, was ensnared in a deep depression since the end of WWI with little hope of escaping the desperate situation. There was among the intelligentsia, an extreme skepticism toward the market economy and capitalism, coupled with great optimism for planning and the promise of socialism. British intellectuals in the 1930s, such as Harold Laski and William Beveridge, were dedicated social reformers. They despaired over the social costs they identified with unbridled capitalism resulting from monopoly power, externalities, macroeconomic volatility, mass unemployment, and income inequality.

This attitude was shared widely among the cultural elites. Harold Laski (1942, p. 111), perhaps the most famous public intellectual in the English-speaking world at the time, argued in a Labor Party document "A Planned Economic Democracy" that: "Nationalization of the essential instruments of production before the war ends, the maintenance of control over production and distribution after the war – this is the spearhead of this resolution." Any objection to these plans and policy promises were dismissed as relics of an illusionary age of *laissez-faire*. But such dogmatic "Manchesterism" was refuted as a governing ideology ever since at least Keynes's "End of Laissez-Faire" ([1926] 1978). This rejection of *laissez-faire* was not in the minds of most British intellectuals aligned with a rejection of the values of democracy and the rule of law. The old liberalism was in crisis, but a new liberalism could fulfill the promise. *It is critically important to understand for contextualizing the reception of Hayek's argument when it was offered to the public and the*

---

[4] This shared perspective can also be seen in their respective correspondence in the 1930s with Walter Lippmann prior and immediately after the publication of *The Good Society* (1937). See Boettke and Candela (2019) for a discussion.

profession, that from the perspective of British intellectuals, they firmly believed that they were socialists in their economics precisely because they were liberal democrats in their politics.[5]

Hayek had heard all this before in the coffee houses of Vienna and throughout German language periodicals. He decided he had to try to offer a warning to his sincere colleagues and fellow liberal democrats who were confused.[6] *The Road to Serfdom* ([1944] 2007) was the result of that effort and was published in the UK in March 1944 and the US in September 1944. Hayek's life would never be the same, and one could reasonably argue that neither would the world of ideas and public policy.

Hayek sought to demonstrate the incompatibility of socialist economic policy with the rule of law and democracy.[7] Key to his argument is that in a democratic liberal society, there's no overarching single scale of values. Society cannot achieve a single hierarchy of ends we all agree on.[8] In fact, the great strength of democratic liberal societies is the great multiplicity of values that are respected among diverse, often divergent, and physically and socially distant individuals. Liberal democratic society is a pluralistic society. As a result, there are severe limits of agreement on *ends* within a functioning democratic society, and thus we must restrain ourselves if we are to remain a liberal democracy to an agreement on the *means* by which we interact, resolve our conflicts, and come eventually to live better together. Democracy is a way to relate to one another as dignified equals – not simply as a set of voting procedures – and liberalism is the broader set of guiding principles for the institutional infrastructure of a society of free and responsible individuals.

In *The Road to Serfdom*, Hayek deploys economic analysis to address the institutional questions that real-world socialist economies would need to face, the organizational logic of socialist planning, and the logic of the situation that socialist decision-makers must confront. The organizational and situational logic that socialist planning would follow is such that democracy and the rule of law are unsustainable in any substantive content, and the system, if pursued

---

[5] Perhaps the best book that captures this conviction is Durbin's *New Jerusalems: The Labor Party and the Economics of Democratic Socialism* (1985).

[6] Hayek writing to his old Viennese friend Fritz Machlup 31 July 1941 states his motivation for putting aside his work on scientism and working on this new book aimed at a more popular audience: "If one cannot fight the Nazis one ought least to fight the ideas which produced Nazism" (quoted in Hayek 2018, p. 319).

[7] Hayek had earlier sketched out this argument in his essay "Freedom and the Economic System" (Hayek [1938] 2012)

[8] This is not the place to pursue this point, but Hayek in making this argument does anticipate Arrow's impossibility argument about preference aggregation *via* democratic procedures, and Buchanan's critique of social welfare economics. Some implications of this are discussed in Boettke and Leeson (2002).

to its logical end, would result in the concentration of political power in the hands of men least capable of constraining the abuse of that power. The worst of us will end up on top, a result confirmed by the coincidence of the three leading political mass murders of the twentieth century rising to the top of socialist systems – Hitler, Stalin, Mao. Hayek's argument, as we have seen, is not an argument of inevitability, but merely a simple application of the principle of comparative advantage to the realm of politics, particularly when politics is demanding such a comprehensive command and control stance to be taken by those in leadership. "Just as the democratic statesman who sets out to plan economic life will soon be confronted with the alternative of either assuming dictatorial powers or abandoning his plans," Hayek tells his reader, "so the totalitarian dictator would soon have to choose between disregard of ordinary morals or failure. It is for this reason that the unscrupulous and uninhibited are likely to be more successful in a society tending toward totalitarianism." ([1944] 2007, p. 158)

Hayek further makes this point when he argues that "whoever controls all economic activity controls the means for all our ends and must therefore decide which are to be satisfied and which not" ([1944] 2007, p. 126). Therefore, Hayek warns his friends – those socialists of all parties – that "democratic socialism, the great utopia of the last few generations, is not only unachievable, but that to strive for it produces something so utterly different that few of those who now wish it would be prepared to accept the consequences, many will not believe until the connection has been laid bare in all its aspects" ([1944] 2007, p. 82). Laying bare the *logical* (though not necessarily inevitable) consequences for liberal democracy of socialist economic policy is what Hayek set out to do. The result of pursuing this policy path of planning to its logical conclusion is a grotesque distortion of the democratic liberal vision of society, and all the more tragic is that it was pursued with the most sincere and best of intentions. "Is there a greater tragedy imaginable," Hayek asks, "than that, in our endeavor consciously to shape our future in accordance with high ideals, we should in fact unwittingly produce the very opposite of what we have been striving for?" ([1944] 2007, p. 60).

It's critically important to understand, however, that Hayek's argument in *The Road to Serfdom* was never a slippery slope argument, as critics often suggest. Hayek pursues a situational logic grounded in the *economic analysis of socialist economic planning*. Such an analysis, as we have been stressing, is strictly speaking value-free, and simply explores the coherence of chosen means to the achievement of given ends. If economic analysis can demonstrate that economic planners are pursuing goals which the policies pursued cannot in fact achieve, yet they insist on pursuing anyway, the resulting order will be defined by unintended and undesirable consequences of economic deprivation and political tyranny. *The Road to Serfdom* in this sense is an "autopsy" of the political-economy corpse of the persistent pursuit of a false utopia. But there is nothing inevitable about such a persistent pursuit by the ruling elite in any society. Crucially, as the frustrating feedback is produced by the failed effort at socialist economic planning, it's up to those in positions of power to decide to continue down a predetermined road or to change path. If they change the path, then tragedy can be avoided. If Hayek's warning is not heeded, then this tragedy unfolds as the logic of choice feeds into a situational logic of the socialist aspiration. Neither economic development nor political freedom results from socialist economic planning. Along the pathway to a New Jerusalem, a New Serfdom results instead of what was promised.

It's a warning that, if heeded, means that the road where the danger to our freedom lies can be avoided. For many years, countries such as the UK and the Nordic states made the turn down that road, but their leaders exited under the influence of Hayek's admonition. But those turns were decades after Hayek wrote. In real time, Hayek dedicated his book "To the socialists of all parties." This was not meant as an ironic jab, but as a sincere offering. Hayek was not morally objecting to the desired ends of the socialist aspirations to address the social ills of his time.[9] His objection was, as it was for his mentor Ludwig von Mises (1920, 1922, 1949) before him, that the socialist means were incapable of producing those desired ends. Addressing poverty, ignorance, and squalor, and countering monopoly power, and macroeconomic volatility, was every bit as pressing in Hayek's political economy as those of his socialist colleagues at the LSE and elsewhere.

3.3 Misunderstandings of Economists

E. F. Durbin's review article on *The Road to Serfdom* stated that Hayek was wrong because "[w]e all wish to live in a community that is as rich as possible, in which consumers' preferences determine the relative output of goods that can be consumed by individuals, and in which there is freedom of discussion and political association and responsible government," but "[m]ost of us are social-ist in our economics because we are "liberal" in our philosophy" (Durbin 1945, p. 357).

---

[9] Hayek, we contend, was seeking what Lavoie would describe as true radical liberalism in *National Economic Planning: What is Left?* and a version of what Hodgson describes in *Liberal Solidarity* (2021). There is nothing atomistic about Hayek's vision, nor status quo preserving and conservative. Among contemporary works, perhaps Deirdre McCloskey's *Why Liberalism Works* (2019) represents the best statement of that vision of economic, political, and social life.

It is our contention that Durbin went down this argumentative alley because (a) he misinterpreted Hayek as having abandoned Mises's "impossibility of rational economic calculation" thesis, and (b) misread Hayek as making a slippery slope argument rather than what we will call the "instability" argument. In focusing his critique through this distorted interpretative framing, Durbin and others were led to ignore the institutional weakness of the socialist proposals. As Hayek argues the decision authority must choose to go further along the amassing of centralized power, or abandon the policy agenda being pursued (Boettke 2005, p. 1048; Boettke and Candela 2017).

There simply is no ironclad inevitability in Hayek's argument, as presented in *The Road to Serfdom*. The argument, instead, is a warning of a tragic possibility that would be viewed as abhorrent from the point of view of those who believe they are "socialists in their economics because they are liberals in their philosophy." What Hayek was addressing to socialists of the time, particularly in England, was the lagging link between socialist ideas and how such socialist ideas would later demand institutional changes that are inconsistent with liberal principles, transforming democratic institutions into instruments of totalitarian rule:

> I know that many of my Anglo-Saxon friends have sometimes been shocked by the semi-Fascist views they would occasionally hear expressed by German refugees, whose genuinely socialist convictions could not be doubted. But while these observers put this down to the others' being Germans, the true explanation is that they were socialists whose experience had carried them several stages beyond that yet reached by socialists in England and America. It is true, of course, that German socialists have found much support in their country from certain features of the Prussian tradition ... But it would be a mistake to believe that the specific German rather than the socialist element produced totalitarianism. It was the prevalence of socialist views and not Prussianism that Germany had in common with Italy and Russia – and it was from the masses and not from the classes steeped in the Prussian tradition, and favored by it, that National-Socialism arose. (Hayek [1944] 2007, pp. 62–63)

The connections that Hayek said must be laid bare is the link between the organizational logic of socialist planning and the situational logic of political decision-making under socialism against the backdrop of Mises's impossibility thesis. The market socialist writers of the 1930s and 1940s were ignoring the connections Hayek was attempting to get them to see. They were instead myopically pursuing economic reasoning as if institutions did not matter, and that resource decisions were purely technical ones.

3.4 The Socialist Response

In his gentlemanly critique of Hayek's *The Road to Serfdom*, A. C. Pigou (1944) writes that Hayek raises good points, is a careful economic thinker, and presents his ideas in effective prose. However, Pigou then misrepresents the book by arguing that Hayek's position is that liberty and responsibility are ends not to be bargained away, even if in bartering we could increase economic satisfaction by eradicating social ills. This, of course, is decidedly *not* Hayek's position. The tragedy Hayek warns about in *The Road to Serfdom* is that people have traded away their economic liberties in the hope of addressing social ills and protecting their political liberties. But in pursuing this path, they instead experience exacerbated social ills *and* incur a loss of political liberties. That is why it is a tragic tale. Pigou's discussion simply misses the means-ends analysis of economic reasoning championed by Mises and Hayek in their discussion of the problems of economic policy design.

One of the most interesting positions in the discussion is put forth by E. R. Durbin. He argues that Hayek has abandoned economic theory for a strange psychology (Durbin 1945). What he means is that Hayek is making an incentive-based argument, that Durbin (and others such as Oskar Lange 1937, p. 127) argued was out of bounds in sophisticated theoretical discussions in economics. The argument made was two-fold: (a) theory should be context-*independent*, and (b) methodologically incentive-based arguments violated the strict adherence to value-freedom in the analysis of economic systems by postulating that actors may not have the public interest in mind. Durbin (and Lange) confused questions of motivation with the analysis of systemic incentives, a common mistake among market socialists at the time. In fact, in Durbin's archives at the LSE, in lecture notes for his class on socialist economic planning, he has on page 1 the notation – "No truck with incentive talk."[10]

In addition, Durbin interprets Hayek as making an inevitability and slippery slope argument, and not a cautionary warning about the logic of the situation. Durbin does make the interesting assertion that Hayek abandoned Mises, without really specifying the nature of the abandonment. But if we are permitted to reconstruct his intent from the text, we would suggest that what he means is that, to his mind, Mises said socialism was impossible, while Hayek says it is possible but undesirable. Durbin says that, in *The Road to Serfdom*, instead of

---

[10] The discerning reader would do well to consult Milton Friedman's *Journal of Political Economy* review essay (1947) on Abba Lerner's *The Economics of Control* (1944), in which Friedman grants the competency of Lerner's logically valid deductions, but Friedman challenges the practical relevance of Lerner's analysis precisely because Lerner nowhere addresses the problems associated with the administration of the various public policies advocated by real human beings.

Mises's incorrect but logical argument, we get a dubious psychological and politically dogmatic argument. Durbin also claims Hayek is anti-science because of his critique of what would later be known as rational constructivism. And in the end, Hayek is ultimately wrong because he doesn't understand that British intellectuals and British culture will never let planning undermine liberal traditions (Durbin 1945). That might have happened in Germany, but never in Britain.

This pattern is reflected in most of the main professional reviews of *The Road to Serfdom*, and continued with the way Paul Samuelson presented the thesis of the book in his best-selling textbook, *Economics*.[11] Focusing mainly on Durbin and the other market socialists of the 1930s and 1940s, one sees that there is a serious error of omission in the debate. The economic problems and the political problems go missing in the discussion by assumption, producing an intellectual impasse, which in many ways persists to this day.

3.5 Market Socialism

It was simply a matter of mathematical logic that if the socialist system was to achieve advanced material production, the formal conditions of economic efficiency stipulated by marginalist principles had to be satisfied. Economists *across the ideological spectrum* from the US and the UK, such as Frederick Taylor (1929), Frank Knight (1936), H. D. Dickinson (1933), Joseph Schumpeter (1942), Oskar Lange (1936, 1937), and Abba Lerner (1934, 1935, 1936) began developing an argument based on a *common methodological starting point*: they used modern neoclassical economics to ensure the efficiency of socialist economic planning. Using neoclassical reasoning, Oskar Lange believed he was able to formulate a definitive critique of Mises based on the formal similarity of equilibrium conditions under both capitalism and socialism.

It is important to emphasize that the formal similarity argument was laid out clearly by Frederick Wieser (1893), and as Hayek stressed, Mises (and other critics of socialism) never said that these formal principles shouldn't be met. In fact, they argued that they should. The question was whether they could ever be satisfied in the absence of a private-property market economy with its relative prices and profit-and-loss accounting. Nevertheless, deploying the formal similarity argument, Lange provided the following blueprint. First, allow a market for consumer goods and labor allocation. Second, put the productive sector into

---

[11] See Farrant and McPhail (2010) on the discussion of the correspondence between Hayek and Samuelson on what Hayek considered Samuelson's misrepresentation of his argument from *The Road to Serfdom*.

state hands but provide strict production guidelines to firms. Namely, inform managers that they must price their output equal to marginal costs, and produce that level of output that minimizes average costs. Adjustments can be made on a trial-and-error basis, using inventory as the signal. The production guidelines will ensure that the full opportunity cost of production will be taken into account and that all least-cost technologies will be employed. In short, these production guidelines will ensure that productive efficiency is achieved even in a setting of state ownership of the means of production (Lange 1936).

Lange argued that not only is socialism theoretically capable of achieving the same level of efficient production as the market, but it would actually outperform capitalism by purging society of monopoly and business cycles that plague real-world capitalism. Moreover, since the means of production would rest in the hands of authorities, market socialism would also be able to pursue egalitarian distributions in a manner unobtainable with private ownership. In the hands of Lange (and Lerner 1937), neoclassical theory was to become a powerful tool of social control. Modern economic theory, which Mises and Hayek had thought so convincingly established their argument, was now used to show that they were wrong. But this showed a fundamental flaw in the evolution of modern economic theory. As Hayek would say in the last paragraph of his famous essay "The Use of Knowledge in Society" (1945), when habits of thought mislead even the profession's brightest minds into committing fundamental errors, something is amiss. What was amiss was confusion over the purpose of the theory of static equilibrium in economic science.

Lange's model of market socialism presented a formidable challenge for believers in the productive superiority of capitalism, a challenge that Hayek would devote the better part of the 1940s attempting to meet.[12] Hayek's response to the arguments for market socialism came in the form of a multi-pronged attack. First, Hayek argued that the models of market socialism proposed by Lange and others reflected a preoccupation with equilibrium. The models possessed no ability to discuss the necessary adaptations to changing conditions required in real economic life. The imputation of the value of capital goods from consumer goods represented a classic case in point. Schumpeter (1942, p. 175) argued that once consumer goods were valued in the market (as they would be in Lange's model), a market for producer goods was unnecessary because we could impute the value of corresponding capital goods *ipso facto*. Within the framework of equilibrium analysis, the Lange–Lerner conditions

---

[12] Hayek's essays are collected in Hayek (1948). See Caldwell (1997) for a discussion of the development of Hayek's thought that was brought on by his debate over socialism.

would hold – prices would be set to marginal cost (and thus the full opportunity cost of production would be reflected in the price) and production would be at the minimum point on the firm's average cost curve (and thus the least-cost technologies would be employed). But what, Hayek asked, do these conditions tell us about a world where the data are not frozen? What happens when tastes and technologies change? If everyone is a passive price taker in a world of parametric pricing, then how can price setting by a central planner ever reflect the context-specific knowledge embodied in market prices, generated only by active buying and selling? Pricing outside the context of the market process is analogous to knowing the score of a particular sporting match before the game is even played.

The marginal conditions of optimality, Hayek noted, do not provide any guide to action; they are instead outcomes of a process of learning within a competitive situation. In a tautological sense, competition exists in all social settings, and thus individuals find that in order to do the best they can given their situation, they will stumble towards equating marginal costs and marginal benefits. This is true at the individual level no matter what system we are talking about. But this says nothing about the first optimality rule proposed in the Lange–Lerner model – that of setting price equal to marginal cost – nor does it address the second optimality rule of the model – that of producing at the level which minimizes average costs. Both rules are definitions of an end point in a certain competitive process, not guiding rules for actors within that process. Rather than being given to us from above, entrepreneurs must discover anew each day what the best price to offer is, what the least-cost methods of production are, and how best to satisfy consumer tastes.

3.6 Problems of Dynamic Coordination

This "solution" was of course accurate in the model of general equilibrium where there is a pre-reconciliation of plans (i.e., no false trades) as a characteristic of the model. Hayek's concern, however (like Mises's) was not with the model of general equilibrium, but with how imputation actually takes place within the market process so that production plans come to be coordinated with consumer demands through time. This is not a trivial procedure and requires various market signals to guide entrepreneurs in their decision process on the use of capital good combinations in production projects. In a fundamental sense, Hayek's central point was that Mises's calculation argument could not be addressed by assuming it away. Of course, if we focus our analytical attention on the properties of a world in which all plans have already been fully coordinated (general competitive equilibrium), then the process by which that coordination came about in the first place will not be highlighted since the process will have already been worked out by assumption.

Hayek argued that this constituted the missing economics in the argument over socialist planning. Absent certain institutions and practices, the process that brings about the coordination of plans (including the imputation of value from consumer goods to producer goods) would not take place. In other words, the *ipso facto* proposition that would hold in competitive equilibrium was irrelevant for the world outside of that state of equilibrium. The fact that leading neoclassical economists (like Knight and Schumpeter) had not recognized this elementary point demonstrated the havoc that a preoccupation with the static state of equilibrium, as opposed to the process which tends to bring about equilibrium, can have on economic science.

An institutionally antiseptic economics did not advance economic science. Instead, one could argue it was a block to progress in science, as argued by Kenneth Boulding (1948), the second recipient of the John Bates Clark Medal, in his review essay on Samuelson's *Foundations of Economic Analysis* (1947). Boulding understood the dangers that historicism and old institutionalism represented to the advancement of economic science. He appreciated that theoretical rigor could help clear up many endless debates that had plagued political economy from the classics to the moderns. Confusion results when we use the same words to mean different things, and different words to mean the same thing. Mathematics has the ability to cut through that confusion, but, as Boulding warned, "the greatest danger is from the other side. The mathematicians themselves set up standards of generality and elegance in their expositions which are a serious bar to understanding" and "it may well be that the slovenly literary borderland between economics and sociology will be the most fruitful building ground during the years to come and that mathematical economics will remain too flawless in its perfection to be very fruitful" (Boulding 1948, p. 199).

That slovenly literary borderland between economics and sociology is what Weber, Schumpeter, and Mises called sociology and today we might call economic sociology. It is the ground where the economic calculus of individual decision-making is recognized to always take place against a backdrop of political, legal, and social institutional contexts. The logic of choice of pure theory is transformed into the situational logic of applied theory. By draining economics of the institutional context in the striving for mathematical elegance, the mid-century synthesis derailed the scientific progress that was made by the classical political economists and the early neoclassical economists such as the Austrians, the Swedes such as Wicksell, and British economists such as Wicksteed.

From 1930 to 1960, economic science became dominated by excessive formalism and excessive aggregation, both of which conspired to conceal from analysis the economic process. These developments and the belief in economics as a branch of social engineering led to a naïve embrace of statistical measures to aid the economics of control. In short, the idea of economics as a science of human action and interaction was displaced by a vision of the science as an exercise in modeling and measuring, or as Abba Lerner (1944) would put it, an economics of control.

In Hayek's view, the problem with concentrating on a static state of affairs, as opposed to the processes that produce that state, was not simply limited by a description of formal conditions, but also precluded theoretical attention away from how ever changing circumstances require constant adaptations and adjustments on the part of participants within the economic system to achieve the coordination of plans through time.[13] Equilibrium, by definition, is a state of affairs in which no agent within the system has any incentive to change. If all the data were frozen, then indeed logic would lead individuals to a state of rest where all plans were coordinated and resources were used in the most efficient manner currently known.

Hayek's argument was essentially that we must flip our theoretical priorities. Rather than reject equilibrium theory, to the contrary, he found it foundational to scientific progress. But, to achieve an explanation of how markets work, the priority must be on the processes of exchange and production guided by relative prices, and disciplined by profit-and-loss accounting in our theorizing. Economics is about exchange and the institutions within which exchange takes place, and it is a science of tendencies and directions of change and not exact points of rest. As Hayek stressed throughout his essays in the 1930s and 1940s, the economic problem in society we must address results as a consequence of change. There is no economic problem to study in the static end state of a general competitive equilibrium.

Effective allocation of resources requires that there is a correspondence between the underlying conditions of tastes, technology, and resource endowments, and the induced variables of relative prices, quantities, and methods of production. In perfect competition, the underlying variables and the induced variables are in perfect alignment and thus there are no coordination problems.

---

[13] This point has been recognized not only by John Bates Clark Medalist, Franklin Fisher (1983), but also more recently by Brian Arthur (2023), who has written a fascinating paper on the economics of a world of nouns (neo-classical economics) and economics appropriate for a world of verbs (emergent order economics). This, we believe, is a useful way to think about what Hayek was arguing in the 1930s and 1940s in his essays on price system and the competitive order.

Traditions in economic scholarship that reject the self-regulation proposition tend to deny that there is any correspondence between the underlying conditions and the induced variables in the market. According to Hayek, the market-process approach avoids these polar extremes and instead is characterized by focusing our analytical attention on the constant adapting and readapting by economic actors to the changing circumstances guided by relative prices, lured by profits, and penalized by losses.

3.7 Hayek's Critique of the Market Socialists

Hayek, in contrast to both of these alternatives, sought to explain the lag between the underlying and the induced. Economics for him is a science of tendency and direction, not one of exact determination. Changes in the underlying conditions set in motion accommodating adjustments that are reflected in the induced variables on the market. The induced variables lag behind, but are continually pulled toward the underlying conditions.[14]

The detour into equilibrium and away from a focus on equilibration at the core of economic theory was important because of the turn the debate took after Lange's paper and the transformation of the basic language in economics. To the Austrians Mises and Hayek, *disequilibrium* prices play a critical role in the social epistemics of the complex coordination of economic activity through time. The relevant knowledge that is dispersed throughout the system must be discovered, communicated, and utilized by decision-makers acting within specific contexts. The knowledge problem that Hayek identified related to this context-specific nature of knowledge. Outside that context, it is not that the knowledge is difficult to gather but that it ***does not exist***, for it is only in that context and through the exchange and production activities within that context that the knowledge is generated in the first place. This is the meaning of Hayek's knowledge of "time and place." None of these aspects of the price system are addressed in the Lange model. For Lange and mathematical neoclassical economists, prices represent a sufficient statistic for a competitive equilibrium solution.

Hayek's fundamental critique of Lange's contribution was that economists ought not to assume what they must in fact demonstrate for their argument to hold. Informational assumptions were particularly problematic in this regard. As Hayek developed his argument, he for the most part steered clear of motivational issues and claimed that individuals (both privately and as planners) would have only the best of intentions. However, while assuming moral

---

[14] Kirzner (1992) provides perhaps the most thorough discussion of this vision of the market process.

perfection, like Mises, he refused to assume intellectual perfection. This was quite understandable. If one assumes both moral and intellectual perfection, then what possible objection could anyone raise to the rational planning of the economic system? In line with our discussion about equilibration vs. equilibrium, Hayek argues that perfect knowledge is a defining characteristic of the equilibrium end state, but cannot be an assumption within the process of equilibration. The question instead is: how do individuals come to learn the information that it is necessary for them to have in order to coordinate their plans with others?

In "Economics and Knowledge" (1937) and "The Use of Knowledge in Society" (1945), Hayek develops the argument that the way in which economic agents come to learn represents the crucial empirical element of economics, and that price signals represent the key institutional guidepost for learning within the market process. Traditional neoclassical theory taught that prices were incentive devices, which indeed they are. But Hayek pointed out that prices also serve an informational role, which is, unfortunately, often overlooked. *Prices serve this communicative role by economizing on the amount of information that market participants must process and by translating the subjective trade-offs that other participants make into "objective" information that others can use in formulating and carrying out their plans.*

As the debate progressed, Hayek emphasized different aspects of this argument, placing particular emphasis on the contextual nature of the knowledge that is utilized within the market process. Knowledge, he pointed out, does not exist disembodied from the context of its discovery and use. Economic participants base their actions on concrete knowledge of a particular time and place. This local knowledge that market participants utilize in orienting their actions is simply not abstract and objective and thus is incapable of being used by planners outside that context to plan the large-scale organization of society.

Hayek's reasons for holding that planning cannot work are not limited to the problem that the information required for the task of coordinating the plans of a multitude of individuals is too vast to organize effectively. His point is *not* a computational one. Instead, Hayek argued that the knowledge utilized within the market by entrepreneurs *does not exist* outside that local context and thus cannot even be organized in principle. It is not that planners would face a complex computational task; it is that they face an *impossible* task because the knowledge required is not accessible to them no matter what technological developments may come along to ease the computational burden. The relevant knowledge of the market is generated within a context; absent that context it is not generated.

According to Hayek, the central question for understanding social order is "not how we can "find" the people who know best, but rather what institutional arrangements are necessary in order that the unknown persons who have knowledge specially suited to a particular task are most likely to be attracted to that task" (1948, p. 95). Missing the subtle issues in economic theory was only one issue; Hayek also was appalled that his colleagues at the LSE and elsewhere were increasingly failing to acknowledge the essential political, legal, and social framework within which economic life exists. Economic science is about exchange and the institutions within which exchange takes place. In subsequent decades, Hayek would identify that the same root methodological error that led to the missing economics would also be responsible for the missing institutions. But for our purposes here, what matters is that Hayek had to stress to his colleagues the classical political economists' insights that the institutions of private property, contract, and consent, embedded in a system of general rules that protect these institutions, are crucial not only to mobilizing incentives but also in ensuring that economic actors are able to utilize their individual knowledge of time and place in making decisions in such a way that their plans may be coordinated, and productive specialization and peaceful social cooperation will be realized. These institutions Hayek cites are precisely the institutions of liberalism – private property and freedom of contract protected under a rule of law.[15]

4 The End of the Debate? Lavoie's Challenge and the Fall of Communism

4.1 Mid-century Economics

As the twentieth century moved into its latter half, the debate stalled. Despite clearly unaddressed points raised by Mises and Hayek, the economics profession generally conceded the debate to Lange, Lerner, and the market socialists (see, e.g., Bergson 1948). The reasons for this are undoubtedly manifold, and the sociology of economics is perhaps insufficiently developed to give us a definitive answer as to why the socialist calculation debate was more or less abandoned. But there are two facts to recognize that may give us the perspective of economists circa, say, 1950.

The first is that data (which we now know to have been deeply flawed) seemed to suggest that the Soviet Union – hitherto the greatest, or at least most ambitious, of the socialist experiments – was in fact successful. For instance, GDP figures reported levels of wealth comparable to that in the

---

[15] Again see Robbins (1952) for a discussion of the emphasis on the institutional infrastructure among classical economists.

West. Indeed, until the collapse of the USSR in 1989, Paul Samuelson's classic introductory economics textbook listed this fact alone as a reason to dismiss the arguments of the Austrians (Samuelson and Nordhaus 1989).[16] The apparent economic success of the Soviet Union, as evidenced by per capita GDP, export figures, and great social projects like the Russian space program, revealed to economists that something was wrong with the Austrian point about central planning. The Austrians had argued that socialism would be inefficient; but it clearly wasn't, so the Austrians must be wrong.

The second and related fact is that Mises and Hayek turned their attention to new projects. Put simply, Mises and Hayek had a principled skepticism of the institutionally sterile economic theory of their day, as well as of the ways economists began to employ statistics. They realized that their arguments were not more widely accepted because the now dominant economic theory, in its abstractions for the sake of mathematical tractability, had assumed away the very problems that the Austrians raised. In the welfare economics of the time, for example, a benevolent planner would simply maximize the social welfare function that was given. What was the problem? Moreover, the increasing reliance on data such as GDP figures was in their minds misleading. Modern economics, to Mises and Hayek, had a formalism problem and an aggregation problem, and both problems conspired to distort economists' appreciation for the complex coordination of a market economy. They thus sought to articulate their methodological differences, so that the profession might more clearly understand the nature of the calculation argument.

Planners cannot simply direct firms to price at marginal costs, because the marginal costs of production are not a given. Marginal costs must be discovered, and discovered anew each day in response to changing local conditions. Prices capture this dispersed and, importantly, often tacit knowledge, and communicate this knowledge to firms. Superseding the price mechanism stifles the discovery process. Data is no help here, for data speaks of averages and aggregates and thus abstracts away from local conditions. For Hayek, prices capture and communicate knowledge which is not communicable as data, and which is not "given" in any helpful sense.

4.2 The Austrians Turn to Methodology

It is clear that this frame of thinking represents an important departure from the conventional assumptions of contemporary economic theory, where marginal costs are given and firms simply confront an optimization problem. For Hayek,

---

[16] See Levy and Peart (2011) on the overestimation of Soviet growth in American economics textbooks.

it is not wrong *per se* to speak of optimization, but it is deeply misguided to think that the stylized optimization problems in textbook models describe the totality of the market. Thus, Hayek and Mises turned to the task of clarifying their methodological differences. The task at hand became not the refutation of socialism by economic theory, but the improvement of economic theory such that their concerns about socialism could be communicated in the first place. The Austrians were tragically maligned as ideologues for this move, a record which has fortunately been set straight in recent scholarship (Wasserman 2019; Dekker 2016). It was sometimes unfairly thought of Mises and Hayek that their methodological arguments were mere quibbles to defend a kind of "market fundamentalism." Rather, as we have seen, the Austrians had a point about the nature of knowledge and the operation of the market process they wanted to make, and which then-contemporary economic theory prevented them from making.

Thus, Hayek turned to his (ultimately aborted) project "Studies on the Abuse and Decline of Reason" and published *The Counter-Revolution of Science* (1952). Mises, for his part, translated into English his treatise and published it as *Human Action* (1949), wherein he summarized the major arguments of his career thus far: not only the calculation argument and his theory of the entrepreneurial market process, but also his methodological concerns, alongside his business cycle theory, and his analysis of interventionism as well as a defense of liberalism. In his analysis of bureaucracy and government policy, Mises one could argue also pioneered an inquiry into nonmarket decision-making. He followed up *Human Action* with *Theory and History* (1957) and translated and released an English edition of *Epistemological Problems of Economics* (1960), both of which addressed the methods of the human sciences at their core and drew connections between the methodological disputes and the calculation debate.

For whatever reason – and again, there are probably many – economics as a profession did not follow Mises and Hayek into their methodological investigations. In a sense, Hayek was seen as abandoning economics and becoming a public philosopher, and in his attempts to articulate a positive vision of liberty and resuscitate a non-technocratic social science which accurately grasped the problems with which it wrestled, and this was perhaps a move beyond where many practicing economists could follow. Mises passed away in 1973 during something of an Austrian dark age: economists seemed to have forgotten the calculation debate and the business cycle theory of Mises and Hayek and did not adequately attend to their methodological inquiries.

Be that as it may, the Nobel Prize was awarded to Hayek the following year. Something of a revival in Austrian thought occurred within academic economics (see Vaughn 1994). We have not the space to discuss this at length, but notable figures who transmitted and developed the insights of Mises and Hayek during this time were Israel Kirzner (1973, 1988), Ludwig Lachmann (1977), Karen Vaughn (1980), Dominick Armentano (1969), and Murray Rothbard (1962). Fellow travelers – those who were influenced by or had come to similar conclusions as the Austrians – included Armen Alchian, James Buchanan, Ronald Coase, Harold Demsetz, and Gordon Tullock (see Section 5).

4.3 Don Lavoie Revives the Debate

It was in the wake of this revival in the Austrian School of Economics that the calculation debate was reopened. Donald Lavoie earned his PhD in economics in 1981 from New York University, where he had studied under Kirzner. He began teaching at George Mason University that same year. Lavoie grasped the essence of the calculation argument perhaps better than anyone since Mises and Hayek. He was aided in his understanding by his methodological convictions: he had closely followed the twentieth-century transformations in philosophy of science and was profoundly influenced by Michael Polanyi and the "Growth of Knowledge" literature in the philosophy of science. In 1985, Lavoie published *Rivalry and Central Planning* which summarized the calculation debate in greater detail than we have earlier. He thus presented a forceful argument that "[Mises's initial] challenge was never met" (1985a, p. 183). Thus, socialists yet needed to address the question: how can resourced be rationally allocated without recourse to prices?

Lavoie's book was a success, no doubt aided by the time of its publication. By 1985, word had unequivocally reached the West that the Soviet economy was in shambles. Meanwhile, socialist regimes across the world were undertaking steps to make themselves decidedly less socialist. Gorbachev began perestroika, Hungary and Poland had begun privatization, and reforms were well under way in Deng's China. As economists witnessed the collapse of socialism and the apparent triumph of a new, global liberalism, many wondered why socialism failed so utterly. Lavoie, in his novel presentation of Mises's and Hayek's fifty+-year-old arguments, gave them an answer.

Many, if not most, economists were impacted by the arguments of the calculation debate. Those who retained socialist sympathies were persuaded nonetheless that further work was necessary to render their position credible. The debate was reignited; socialists were once more put on the defensive, attempting for the first time since Lange and Lerner to offer a novel response. Meanwhile, the empirical consensus about the status of Soviet economic growth broke. New research piled up, highlighting pervasive shortages under Soviet socialism. The failure of the Soviet economy, coupled with economic reforms of the 1980s and 1990s in China and throughout the former Soviet bloc, presented a convincing picture to economists in the years following Lavoie's publication that the Austrians had raised a challenge which no one had yet answered. Moreover, the debate spread beyond the boundaries of economics into political economy and social philosophy.

Socialists consistently began to moderate their claims. They aimed no longer at the total central control of all capital, but rather, new variants of "market socialism" in the tradition of Lange and Lerner were devised. These new variants tended to advocate for models of market socialism that marginally substituted a little more of socialism for a little more market. We highlight some examples later.

4.4 Socialist Responses

Bardhan and Roemer (1992) outline a system of "competitive socialism" which would maintain state ownership of capital while devolving the level of administrative control to more local authorities. They propose a "clamshell" economy, where citizens all receive equal endowments of vouchers denominated in "clamshells," not money, which can be used to purchase shares in mutual funds. Shares in mutual funds cannot be purchased with money, but only clamshells, and the clamshells cannot be purchased with money either. Shares in mutual funds are tradeable for other shares in different mutual funds, but nonsalable; that is, a person cannot cash out his mutual funds. Individual stocks can only be traded by the banks who own the mutual funds. If a firm performs poorly, banks who own shares in that company will drop them from their mutual funds. Allowing banks to buy and sell stocks is supposed to preserve the knowledge-generating properties of the price mechanism; prohibiting everyone else from trading stocks directly is supposed to prevent the agglomeration of stocks into the hands of a small, self-perpetuating, elite capitalist class. While we believe there are severe problems with this kind of modified market socialism, some of which we will discuss later, we want to first appreciate the fact that Bardhan and Roemer (1992) take a truly novel step in the theory of socialism. Unfortunately, the authors fail to cite much of the relevant work coming from the calculation debate (including either Mises or Hayek); their lack of effective direct response limits their persuasiveness.

Adaman and Devine (1996, p. 524) offer another exemplar of scholarship furthering socialist theory, this time seeking to offer "an explicit response to the Austrian challenge." Adaman and Devine are further to be commended for understanding the sharp, methodological distinction – notable primarily in rival ways that Austrians and neoclassicals conceptualize the market – which had developed out of the calculation debate. Relying precisely on these Austrian insights, they seek to develop a putatively "Austrian market socialist project" (Adaman and Devine 1996, p. 527). Marxist economist Maurice Dobb similarly criticized neoclassical socialists for concerning themselves too heavily with problems of static efficiencies, to the neglect of more important dynamic concerns. Dobb thought markets tended to be dynamically troubled on account of macroeconomic instability: the decisions of any given firm are bound to be short-sighted since they do not know what other firms will do, and thus are deeply ignorant of future states of the world beyond a very short time-horizon. Central planning overcomes this problem. Adaman and Devine seek to wed the Dobbsian critique of markets to the Austrian critique of neoclassical socialists and proffer a model of "participatory planning," which "seeks to combine planning with the articulation of tacit knowledge" (Adaman and Devine 1996, p. 531). Unfortunately, "participatory planning" amounts to little more than a set of idealized goals, where "negotiation" takes the place of prices and "all relevant information" is made, through some unspecified mechanism, publicly available.

4.5 Modern Austrian Critiques of the New Socialists

Lavoie himself implicitly addressed these and others of the disillusioned radicals whose socialist hopes were dashed in the 80s. His companion 1985 work *National Economic Planning: What is Left?* asks – and answers – what the political Left is and ought to be after the sudden realization that the Austrian criticism had to be acknowledged. The problem with half-planning measures, as Lavoie saw it, was that they missed the general implication of the calculation argument. The new market socialist tactic of substituting a little more market for socialism relied on a falsely narrow conception of "markets." The way in which knowledge is discovered systemically through prices does not preclude the possibility of other knowledge-generating systems. Indeed, following Polanyi (1951, 1958), Lavoie uses the example of a community of scientists.

Scientific discovery is not strictly planned, but emerges through the complex interplay of exchanges between individual scientists pursuing their own heuristic visions of the world. Neither is it unregulated, however: scientists very strictly self-regulate their communities by gatekeeping conference attendance, journals, and the like. A community of scientists is thus in this respect rather like a market of entrepreneurs: different people, with different, often contradictory visions of the world, act to the best of their ability to discover truth (either about the natural world or about how to satisfy consumer preferences). Through the interaction process, institutions and norms (money and double-entry bookkeeping; or ethics review boards and peer-reviewed journals) emerge to provide discipline, feedback, and guidance to entrepreneurs and scientists in the discovery process. The attempt to plan science is obviously a mistake, for no one could know in advance what scientists will discover, and thus it is impossible to organize a scientific discipline around such an end. The process must be organic, discovery must be emergent, and decision-making must be polycentric. The case of the market, argues Lavoie, is isomorphic. It is just irrational to direct the market toward particular ends as it is to direct the community of physicists.

It might be objected to this that scientific discovery gets by without the use of prices. We imagine that many of the new market socialists have this idea in mind: they want the marketplace to look more like the university, where the minds of the many and the wise commune and decide on the best plan of action for the use of resources to meet societal goals. In response to this, it might be claimed that, as a matter of fact, science does *not* get by without the use of prices; indeed, all manner of goods in the academy are produced and purchased for money prices. But a more sophisticated response to this kind of thinking can be leveraged from one of the newest contributions to the calculation literature.

Piano and Rouanet (2020) develop a novel formulation of the calculation argument by explicitly drawing on the transaction costs literature, which had developed concurrently with, but separately from, the economic calculation debate. Coase (1937) raises the following question: if prices are so good at coordinating disparate knowledge (by revealing the relative scarcities of inputs), why do firms exist? Why shouldn't we organize all our affairs through spot markets? Firms are, Coase notes, essentially islands of socialism. And socialist theorists frequently referred to the dream of socialism akin to bringing the entire economy under the direction of "one big firm."[17] Firms are places where resources are allocated by directives, not rivalrous bidding and exchange. Firm managers do not have access to internal prices to guide their allocative decisions.

Coase's answer to this question is famous in economics and is one of the major reasons for which he received the Nobel Prize. Firms, he argued, confront "costs of transacting." Using the price system is a costly activity. Negotiating contracts to price every job, every piece of equipment, and every input in a production process at every level would be obviously inefficient. This does not mean that prices have no function. On the contrary, Coase was among the first to recognize Hayek's essential point about the epistemic function of prices.

---

[17] On the boundaries of the firm and the problem of calculation see Rothbard (1962) and Klein (1996). See also Truitt and Burns (forthcoming).

Coase's theory of the firm affirms that knowledge arrived at through the use of the price system is an economic good. Firms will buy this good up to the point where the marginal benefits equal marginal costs: firms expand until the costs of transacting equal the costs of allocating by managerial directives. In other words, Coase tells us that there is an optimal level of economic organization in the firm.

Piano and Rouanet note the obvious relation to the calculation literature (as had many before them) and make explicit a new formulation of Mises's argument. The great error of the socialist economists was to assume that the optimal number of firms is one, and the optimal size of the firm infinite. But this is hardly a benign assumption. The optimal size of the firm is a matter of comparing the costs of organizing to the costs of transaction. These costs, however, cannot be compared if they are not in the form of money prices. Thus, in order to answer the question, "How many firms should there be?" we must have recourse to money prices. The marketplace is a discovery process; its own limits and internal organization are endogenous to that discovery process.

4.6 The Debate Concludes?

Examining the "clamshell economy" or "participatory planning" through this lens reveals the mistake undergirding attempts to revive market socialism. There exists an optimal level of "planning" – of allocation by command – to be done, because always relying on pricing for knowledge is too costly. Pricing itself tells us where that allocation by command ought to be. This is one, of many, reasons why the issue of residual clamancy is so vital to the operation of firms within the market process.[18] But "clamshell socialism" and "participatory planning" both assume, fairly arbitrarily, that vast sectors of economic activity should be centrally planned. It is, however, obviously a mistake to assume that one has identified exactly where the marginal benefit of knowledge generated in the market is outweighed by the marginal cost of transacting. The optimal size of the firm is an emergent property from the fact that firms compete in the marketplace, and are subject to the discipline of profit-and-loss.

Other arguments were levied against the possibility of market socialism by non-economists. For instance, Shapiro (1989) defended the Mises–Hayek position against socialist philosophers in the journal *Social Philosophy and Policy*.

---

[18] Hayek would stress in his work that there are two types of orders: (1) organizations, such as firms, and (2) spontaneous orders. Organizations have a central decision node, whereas spontaneous orders do not. Organizations in this sense have a teleology (a purpose), spontaneous orders have no teleology, they are not end-related, but means-related entities. It is critically important to keep this distinction in mind when discussing social systems of exchange, production and distribution.

N. Scott Arnold (1987a, 1987b, 1987c) and David Schweickart (1987a, 1987b) held a fascinating exchange regarding market socialism's capacity to perpetuate itself. Arnold shows (convincingly, to our minds) that "there would be a strong tendency for market socialism to degenerate into capitalism" (Arnold 1987b, p. 335).

Shleifer and Vishny (1994) show that in democratically controlled market socialist states, if sustained, there would be a tendency to dramatically under-value economic efficiency and that the pursuit of political over economic objectives would be economically crippling. Similarly, Shleifer and Vishny (1992) provide an interest group explanation for the bias in centrally administered prices that gave rise to the pervasive shortages witnessed across socialist regimes. As Levy (1990) argued, these shortages provided a source of rent for those who had control rights over scarce resources. Anderson and Boettke (1997) leverage this rent-seeking narrative to describe the organizational logic of the Soviet-type economy.

Theodore Burczak (2006) offers a fascinating response to the Austrians in *Socialism after Hayek*. He takes up Boettke's (1995) question, "Why are there no Austrian socialists?" As we have maintained in this Element, the calculation problem precludes Austrians from advocating any kind of central planning. But Burczak attempts a way forward. As Peart and Levy (2009, p. 294) summarize, "[t]hough he accepts Hayek's arguments on planning and markets, Burczak is dissatisfied with two aspects of Hayek's work. First, he does not find in Hayek's work any means by which the safety net can be effected. Second, he does not approve of Hayek's own discomfort with democratic politics in pursuit of 'distributive justice.'" Because credit markets fail severely, markets systemically undermine the quality of life for the under-asseted. Burczak suggests that a large, state-provided social safety net, along with state-mandated worker ownership of firms, can create a market that leaves calculability intact while still dramatically curtailing the vagaries of private enterprise.

Economists have responded in numerous ways to Burczak's argument. Peart and Levy (2009, p. 294) acknowledge that "Hayek does not describe how a safety net might come into being in a market economy." However, they note that Adam Smith and others in the classical liberal tradition defend a much more robust conception of sympathy which, if an accurate characterization of humans, would suggest that markets are capable of much more than Burczak credits them.

Burczak's contribution deserves further engagement. As we saw with Foley earlier, the self-management/worker-controlled model of socialism is a promising one to many socialists. David Prychitko (1991; 2002) has devoted considerable energy to addressing workers' self-management in light of the calculation debate. We will have to leave it at that because to pursue further would regrettably take us too far from the task at hand to pursue with the care it deserves right now. But it should be acknowledged that Burczak's work also suggests an evolution in the socialist position. Socialists like Burczak are conceding that, on the most important margin, Mises was right.

These works are some exemplars among literatures that exploded in the wake of the global end of socialism. Economists, if not social scientists more broadly, came generally to the consensus that socialism was not a viable alternative to capitalism as traditionally constructed. Without the knowledge embodied in prices, decision-makers could not hope to lift anyone out of poverty, let alone out-compete the wealth-generating powers of private enterprise. However, times change. Some notion of socialism remained an attractive aspiration for many and thus was the benchmark welfare standard for social theorists even in the wake of the failure of real-existing socialist regimes. In fact, one common theme among intellectuals on the Left in the 1990s and early 2000s was to stress that Marx did not provide us with any explicit guidebook for the socialist future, but he did provide us with a framework for the critical analysis of capitalism. As East and Central Europe and the former Soviet Union experienced the difficulties of the economic, political, and social transitions, the tide of intellectual opinion began to shift. Add to this the disruptions of globalization and the pain of the Global Financial Crisis, and the socialist aspiration for a more just and humane world moved from a normative benchmark to an animating force for practical action. In many ways, we have come full circle back to where Mises began over 100 years ago. In the following section, we explore the thoughts of some contemporary socialists, once again with reference to the thoughts of Mises and Hayek.

5 Socialism in the Twenty-First Century

5.1 The Landscape of Twenty-First Century Socialism

In the years since the revival of the calculation debate, and the vindication of the Austrians, socialism has once again achieved a kind of popular and academic acclaim. There have emerged a small number of what we might call *scientific* socialists. Scientific socialists are those for whom socialism consists of a set of policy ends, namely various forms of equality and material prosperity, which they link theoretically to a particular means, the nationalization of private capital. These socialists are the intellectual children of the socialists of the twentieth century. They believe that putative problems which pervade capitalism – the system of enterprise characterized by the private ownership of capital – can and should be solved by economic planning. These socialists further tend to take the calculation debate very seriously, maintaining that advances in economic theory and technological advances in artificial intelligence enable the rational planning of the economy by a central authority. Machine learning can be used to compute in precise terms, without money prices, the relative scarcities of goods.

Later, we address the insights of the calculation debate to modern socialists. First, we argue that modern computing solutions, such as those proposed which make use of artificial intelligence, cannot solve the calculation problem. Second, we argue that the calculation problem presents a serious challenge for the efficient nationalization of any sort of industry. Thus, socialists of all stripes would do well to pay attention to the history of the socialist calculation debate.

5.2 Computational Socialism: Reviving the Labor Theory of Value

Allin Cottrell and W. Paul Cockshott (1993; see also Cockshott and Cottrell 1993; Cockshott 1990) offered a socialist response to Lavoie. They broadly accept the Austrian interpretation of the calculation debate and reject the kind of neoclassical market socialism put forth by Lange and Lerner. Instead, they advocate for a new kind of market socialism that relies on an updated version of the Marxian labor theory of value. Essentially, units of labor time can be computed and used to determine efficient strategies of production. Units of labor time may thus substitute for the epistemic function performed by prices; with sufficient computing power, the central planners can calculate the lowest labor-time set of inputs to manufacture any given output.

Output is given in the market socialist fashion: laborers are given labor-time certificates which they may use to buy output. Consumer goods are thus subject to market-like supply and demand effects. The central planning board will decide what to produce by seeing how consumers choose to spend their money. They will make errors, of course, from time to time, but Cottrell and Cockshott see no reason to think that such errors will be systematic or any more severe than those that occur from entrepreneurial failures in ordinary capitalist markets. Markets in consumer products tell the state what to produce; extraordinarily precise labor-time calculations by the state reveal the most cost-effective strategy for production. Thus, the state can rationally plan a socialist economy, through the aid of computers which can calculate the optimal allocation of socially necessary labor time. We appreciate the seriousness of Cottrell and Cockshott's project; their willingness to engage with the Austrian critique is helpful and their response is somewhat novel. However, despite its sophistication, their proposal still fails to refute Mises's initial point.

5.3 Inadequacies in Computational Socialism

As noted earlier, in our discussion of Mises's original presentation of the calculation argument, the necessary unit of labor time for production is endogenous to the process of production itself, and thus not at all capable of providing a remotely objective basis for calculation. Production processes are subject to varying returns to scale and confront diminishing marginal returns. This means that the marginal productivity of a unit of labor depends upon the quantity of the good that is to be produced. The quantity of the good to be produced depends further on the demand for the good; the demand curve for a good relates prices to varying quantities. In other words, the quantity of a good to be produced depends on the price it will command.

In a market, production decisions are made by entrepreneurs who compare expected income (given by price per good times the quantity of goods sold) to costs (given by price per input times the number of inputs purchased). Labor is purchased in the same way any other input is purchased. The operators of firms are able to (imperfectly, but reasonably well) anticipate what sorts of goods people want to buy and bid to hire employees who will produce those goods. Importantly, as we discuss in section 2.6, market institutions also provide feedback. If a producer has earned an accounting profit *ex post* then she knows she has purchased resources from where they are less valuable and moved them to a place where they are more valuable. If she earns an accounting loss, then she knows the inverse. Moreover, if she continues to earn losses, she will be forced to leave the business altogether – she won't have the resources at her disposal to compete for inputs. The picture that results is one of dynamic equilibration. The competitive market process is characterized by a constant evolution toward a solution. Markets are always tending toward, but never reaching a final equilibrium. Profit-earners continue to exist, loss-makers drop out, and survivorship is the ultimate selection mechanism in the competitive market (see Alchian 1950).

Money prices enable this equilibration because, even though prices vary with the relative scarcities of goods, the *unit* in which prices are compared remains roughly constant (barring exceptional macroeconomic instability). The unit of labor time, however, is not constant in the same way. Granting Cottrell and Cockshott that labor units of production can be compared across heterogeneous goods, it does not follow that the labor theory of value in production can be rationally wed to a consumer goods market.

The value of the unit of labor time, or the average contribution of each worker to some final output, depends on how much of that output is to be made. How much of that output is to be made depends upon how much consumers wish to buy. How much consumers wish to buy depends partly upon their budget constraint, which is to say, upon how much they have produced – how much income they have received. But how much income they have received depends on their contributions to the final output, which varies, once again, with the quantity of output produced.

To use the units of labor-time as a means of economic calculation endogenizes too much. There can be no objective unit of account under such a regime: the value of labor time is endogenous to the production process. Thus, the planning board does not have access to rational calculation. The only conditions under which socialism could possibly economize as well as markets would be in a state of pure static equilibrium, where all possible production functions and utility functions are known. If either production functions or utility functions change, the planning board receives no feedback. Consumer goods markets will not be rational, since consumers will have no ability to make consumption plans. Price and quantity are no longer mutually determined; price is determined by quantity under the labor/market socialist regime.

A consumer goods market enables equilibrium between supply (given by the state planning board working with technical relationships between inputs and outputs) and demand (given by consumers who spend labor-time vouchers). The labor-time vouchers' worth, however, is determined by the technical relationship between inputs and outputs. In the case of the market, price is mutually determined *with* quantity by supply and demand. In the case of production decisions by the central planning board, price is determined *by* the quantity of the good to be produced. Thus, Cottrell and Cockshott's updated market socialism generates two different "prices," in terms of labor units, for each good, and it is only by some bizarre coincidence that those prices would happen to align for every single good produced. They offer us no mechanism by which the average amount of labor-time required to produce varying quantities of goods will come to equal exactly the average amount of labor-time consumers desire to spend on each of those quantities. They cannot have their cake and eat it too.

5.4 Tacit Knowledge and Economic Calculation

The second objection we wish to raise concerns the nature of knowledge. Hayek (1945) lays out clearly the problem of *tacit* knowledge, knowledge which cannot be articulated but is captured by the price system. Polanyi (1958, 1966) develops the concept of tacit knowledge into a sophisticated epistemology that Lavoie (1985b) leverages, and with which subsequent socialists have not seriously engaged.

Michael Polanyi raises a surprisingly puzzling question for science: how is it that scientific knowledge grows? The problem is that there is not a single method by which new scientific knowledge is introduced. The so-called "scientific method" is a reductionistic account of how real scientists proceed, and anyway, experimental hypothesis testing does not tell the scientist how to generate interesting and important hypotheses to test in the first place. How, wonders Polanyi, do scientists recognize scientific problems?

Polanyi answers that the ability to recognize a problem is a skill, and thus, like any skill, does not develop by means of a fully specifiable or articulable process. Some of those people who are the very best swimmers or cyclists can describe only very loosely what they do with all the different parts of their bodies as they execute such activities, and some of those who can say the most about *how* to swim or ride a bike are rather poor athletes in comparison. It seems impossible that athletic skill or artistic skill could ever be fully summarized verbally in a description of the method, and even if it could be, it seems even less likely that a person could master a skill merely by understanding its exhaustive description. It is not that the method cannot aid in learning, but rather, that method cannot supplant learning; the achievement of a new skill requires the development of some knowledge that cannot be fully articulated.

The ability to recognize problems and their solutions is similarly a skill, and thus can only be grounded tacitly. Polanyi leverages here the age-old Meno Paradox. Polanyi formulates the paradox thus: "[T]o search for the solution to a problem is an absurdity; for either you know what you are looking for, and then there is no problem; or you do not know what you are looking for, and then you cannot expect to find anything" (1966, p. 22). Admitting recognition as a kind of tacit knowledge offers the solution to the paradox. We can find out new things without being able to say what we are trying to find out in advance because we have a faculty that tells us when we've found something out. When we fill in a jigsaw puzzle, we cannot exactly describe the piece we are looking for, but we may know it when we see it. Thus, we know more than we can tell. Scientists rely on this faculty in the formulation of hypotheses. They have reason to believe that a hypothesis is worth the time and effort of investigation on account of their capacity to recognize puzzles, tensions, and surprising implications in theories, despite having no explicit method which generates such recognition. Science is thus a skillful enterprise, requiring practice, not merely book-learning.

The previous digression has profound implications for the calculation debate, as Lavoie (1985b) notes. Production is not organized according to entirely explicit processes. Rather, entrepreneurs *recognize* problems (Kirzner 1973) which they then attempt to solve. This faculty of recognition is, as seen, not reducible to an articulate method. Entrepreneurs can be seen as hypothesis generators Harper (1996). Each venture into the market is a bold and wishful conjecture subject to the refutation of consumer demands. Sometimes entrepreneurs recognize consumer needs that are not being met and move to meet those by creating new goods. Other times entrepreneurs find new, low-cost mechanisms of production that enable arbitrage into new markets. Still other times entrepreneurs find new technologies of organization that enable more production with few inputs. In all of these activities, entrepreneurs rely partially on tacit knowledge.

Central planning, then, even by the aid of powerful machine learning techniques, cannot harness the totality of knowledge that is used in society. Even if all *explicit* information is made known to the planner, the fact that markets employ information which is not and cannot be made explicit means that central planners must make do with less. Centralizing decision-making with respect to resource use means that the amount of *recognition* – of problems and solutions – is reduced, since the number of recognizers falls.

It might be thought that, while the number of faculties of recognition is reduced by the move away from markets to central planning, society's ability to recognize problems is nonetheless improved. By giving decision-making rights to experts, as opposed to disparate market agents, it may be that while *less* tacit knowledge is incorporated into allocative decisions, the expert knowledge is nonetheless sufficient to improve on market outcomes. Hayek (1945), again, has already dealt with this argument. The kind of tacit knowledge relevant to production is frequently highly local; thus, the faculty that recognizes and solves problems is most useful when it is immersed in highly specific conditions of local production. The knowledge of time and place is both generative and contextual; outside the context, it is not generated. Indeed, one important theory of industrial organization (Penrose 1959) sees firms as existing to transmit a kind of institutional knowledge: instruction manuals can only take one so far, and to succeed in business one must at some point become apprenticed to a master of the craft. Thus, we have good reason to think that markets are able to marshal and organize not only more, but better (for the purposes of production) knowledge (see also Nelson and Winter 1982).

There is further no reason to suppose that the capabilities of AI would be better wielded by the central planner than by diverse firms making their own decisions. Again, the number of decision-making nodes positively relates to the amount and quality of knowledge employed. A single planning board with a powerful social-utility-maximizing computer may make decisions with more knowledge than any individual producer in a market, but the sum of producers in the market (who can and might soon be armed with similar computing power) always uses more knowledge than the planner.

5.5 Socialism and Objective Value

As early as 1967, in a book chapter published posthumously, economists, such as Oskar Lange, exuded great optimism in the power of computational technology to overcome the critiques laid by Mises and Hayek, rendering the price mechanism obsolete. As Lange put it, the problem of economic calculation under socialism was simply a matter of feeding data into a computer and to "put the simultaneous equations on an electronic computer and we shall obtain the solution in less than a second. The market process with its cumbersome *tâtonnements* appears old-fashioned. Indeed, it may be considered as a computing device of the pre-electronic age" (emphasis in original; 1967: 158). In more recent years, following the work of Cockshott and Cottrell, other scholars have attempted to detail planning mechanisms that make use of the novel computing power of AI. Consistently, they have failed to appreciate the fact that tacit and local knowledge is captured by the price system and is reduced by the arbitrary reduction of the number of decision-makers who bring their knowledge to bear upon problems. Still, others have tried to avoid problems of calculation by assuming an implausibly high level of preference homogeneity. For example, Samothrakis (2021) argues:

> If one makes the assumption of truly subjective values that vary continuously and are also widely different from person to person, then indeed a market might be able to allocate surpluses somewhat better than a plan. However, if you do accept that the majority of the population shares some similar preference function, at least in their top priorities (e.g. food, shelter, basic communication devices, electricity, health), the argument is nonsensical and applies only to incorporeal beings. Insofar as there are relatively slow changing patterns in consumption, standard machine learning models, combined with one's own predictions can be used to forecast demand.

Samothrakis' position sounds plausible when stated in such terms. But while everyone does, of course, prefer food, shelter, and so on to the absence of such goods, it is also dubious to think that everyone prefers those goods in the same way and on the same margins. Take, for example, shelter. There is not an obvious optimum square footage per household, or per household member, that is homogeneous across all people. Some might prefer to substitute home size for lot size and have a large plot of excludable outdoor space, and some might prefer the opposite. Some might think that smaller houses and lot sizes are preferable, such that more income can be spent elsewhere. Some households might think such amenities as dishwashers are essential, others might prefer a kitchen with more cupboard space. Everyone wants "basic communication devices," but the enormous differences in electronic products and the range of possible preferences with respect to everything from laptop size to internet speed to monthly data allowances renders the proposal of a "similar preference function" highly problematic.

Moreover, it would seem that the "preference function" tends to shift, dramatically and frequently, for most individuals. The changing landscape of the technologically possible means that, while perhaps a person's preference for "basic communication" has remained the same for a few decades, the difference between the landline and the iPhone 13 is such that it is questionable to insist that the demand curve for communication, which Samothrakis is interested in estimating, has remained remotely stable. The constant flux in relative scarcity between goods means that demand curves are constantly shifting on nearly infinitely many margins and to constantly variable degrees. It is not that people's preferences, or utility curves, are bouncing all over the place, but rather that the array of prices and goods consumers confront is variable, which of course produces variation in demand.

The socialist error comes in assuming away the problem by rendering it a computational problem of aggregating exogenous data, rather than *a problem of discovering knowledge that is endogenous to the context of market exchange.* Though responding directly to Lange, Hayek's point about the nature of data is as relevant now as when he wrote "Two Pages of Fiction: The Impossibility of Socialist Calculation" (1982). Hayek argues that there are two senses that we must distinguish when we use the expression "data": "It can be used legitimately either for the assumption, necessarily made hypothetically by the theorist, that certain facts exist which are not known to him, or for the assumption that particular facts will be known to specified persons and will have certain effects on their actions. *But it is an impermissible falsification of the sequence of cause and effect to claim that the 'data' presumed (though not known) by the theorist are also known to some agency without his showing the process by which they will become known to it*" (emphasis added; Hayek 1982, p. 136).

Assuming that there is a static demand curve for every good (including capital goods), or every good for which we want to socialize production, we can estimate the best possible combination of goods to produce. The whole point of the Austrian literature is that an incalculable number of factors are perpetually altering the relative scarcities of goods, in ways that are not fully specifiable in principle, which of course means that the idea of estimating demand curves for planning purposes is ridiculous. The assumption of an absolute, objective unit of value assumes away the fact that the worth of goods is derived from consumers' subjective estimates of utility. The assumption that there exists some homogenous, relatively constant demand for goods like housing rejects the necessity of negotiating trade-offs on multiple margins, and abstracts from the reality that it "applies only to incorporeal beings." And what is true on the demand side, is doubly true on the supply side. Costs of production are again not summaries of previous decisions but reflect possible future alternative use of scarce resources in different production projects. They are discovered anew each day by the managers on the spot, or if they do poorly, alternative ventures that direct those scarce resources toward more valued uses. Innovation, it must be remembered, is not merely a technological question, but an economic one. It is trade-tested innovations that result in wealth creation. Technologically feasible innovations must prove to be economically viable. To sort the economically viable from the set of technological possibilities is the job of economic calculation; if we cannot engage in economic calculation because we have institutionally rendered it nonsensical, then that sorting doesn't take place. No computer algorithm can supplant the ordinary business of economic life in a commercial society.

5.6 "Participatory Planning"

Most recently, Adaman and Devine (2022) have produced an argument calling for a socialist revision of the calculation debate. They offer a model of "participatory planning," to address deficiencies in prior socialist proposals. We appreciate the authors' recognition of our point that "the epistemological critique of the Austrian school based on the tacit nature of knowledge remains as strong as when initially spelled out against the Lange model," (Adaman and Devine 2022, p. 175) though we do ultimately reject their conclusions. Participatory planning advocates a kind of democratic "negotiated coordination." Essentially, Adaman and Devine envision a federated network of meetings, at which everyone has a voice, where production decisions are made. Their reason for preferring such a system comes down to the fact that they believe capitalist competition results in the prioritization of profit over other kinds of social concerns, such as ecological sustainability. If the people who are directly harmed by pollution have a seat at the decision-making table, then production decisions will reflect a more holistic and balanced scale of values which do not prioritize profit at the expense of aesthetic and ethical values. Efficiency, though not unimportant, is but one among many social considerations.

However, Adaman and Devine do not seriously engage with the Austrian literature *after* conceding that the Austrian account provides an important objection to other socialist models. The Austrian account of the epistemic function of prices is very precise: prices communicate knowledge, much of which is tacit, and thus not communicable via speech. Prices coordinate large amounts of disparate, contradictory, local, and fundamentally unspecifiable skill knowledge and allow for a social production and a division of labor on an enormous scale. Adaman and Devine, after recognizing that the nature of production knowledge precludes something like Cockshott and Cottrell's model from being viable, somehow miss the fact that tacit knowledge will be just as impossible to communicate in meetings of democratic bureaucracies.

They further seem to miss the fact that decision-making itself is costly; that is, a society must economize on the production of decisions as it must on anything else. It is not as though sitting in meetings has no opportunity cost. On the contrary, the decision-making costs associated with meetings can be quite large. There is a reason why, for instance, boards of shareholders appoint CEOs. James Buchanan and Gordon Tullock (1962) point out that the external cost of decision-making (the level to which people are dissatisfied with the decision) falls as the criterion for a decision to be reached approaches unanimity, but the decision-making cost (which, at the extreme, is just the inability to make a decision at all) rises with the percentage of stakeholders whose approval is necessary. Again, socialist theorists too often assume away problems with collective action that they obviously cannot if their schemes are to approach any semblance of workability. Adaman and Devine assume that the best way to make decisions is by some form of participatory, localized democracy, whereas in reality such a procedure is probably appropriate for many decisions and prohibitively costly for others. Trade-offs abound in market and nonmarket settings. The beauty of the market is that it not only enables calculation with respect to production decisions, but also that, *via* money prices, a firm can calculate the opportunity cost of different procedures for making decisions. Just as it is a mistake to assume the optimal number of firms is one, so too is it to think that the best method for determining resource allocation is localized democratic meetings.

Last, we would like to point out that market prices surely (though admittedly imperfectly) capture at least some "non-economic" values, like justice, ecological sustainability, and the like, since market prices are partially determined by preferences, and what makes Adaman and Devine's case plausible at all is the fact that we have intuitive moral preferences about the values of things like justice and the environment. In fact, markets help us negotiate the various trade-offs that result from conflicting values by putting a price to some extent on our moral preferences. This makes actors express not their notional demands for vague concepts like ecological sustainability, but act in accordance with their effective demand for concrete ecological decisions. It is not obvious that a burdensome quantity of meetings will capture such values better than, or even as well as, the marketplace in the decisions they reach.

Since Lavoie revived and clarified the Austrian position, the socialist response has not been as robust as one might have expected given the intellectual stakes involved. Arguments should have advanced more than they have. Socialist theorists have expressed their interest in the Austrian literature, cited it at length, and yet have simply failed to internalize the epistemological argument. Central planning's advocates continue to assume away essential features of the economy in their attempt to solve problems with which the price mechanism already deals reasonably well.

5.7 Other Contributions

While we take the literature as being fairly representative of the ongoing discourse, there are a host of contemporary criticisms and defenses of the Austrian calculation argument we have not discussed. We unfortunately cannot address every contribution in detail. However, it should be clear that most of the arguments currently afloat are substantively the same as many of those we have already examined. Nonetheless, we would like to refer the reader to some of the more interesting recent contributions.

Morozov (2019) and King and Petty (2021) defend "technosocialism" achieved through the use of "big data." Boettke and Candela (2023) respond much as we have here, by pointing out that, for the Austrians, the calculation problem is emphatically not a computation problem. The conditions of dynamic uncertainty and tacit knowledge cannot be assumed away. Of course, we could estimate the parameters for a steady-state equilibrium. But we could not rationally decide, based on previous experience alone, what to do with a genuinely novel situation. The competitive market is constantly innovating and never stays still. As William Baumol (2002) argued, the main characteristic of the dynamic capitalist economy is the routinization of innovation. The market is an innovation machine. Novelty is not a question of computability. Neither is the knowledge of time and place that economic actors rely upon in the market to perceive opportunities and act on them. This tacit knowledge cannot be used computationally, since it is by definition inarticulate. Hayek made this argument explicitly in his classic "The Use of Knowledge in Society" (1945), and Lavoie made it a cornerstone of his presentation of the "knowledge problem" in *National Economic Planning* (1985b). We are merely restating its relevance to the discussion in our time concerning technosocialism.

From a more philosophical perspective, Pleasants (1997) offers a Wittgensteinian critique of the concept of tacit knowledge altogether. He views the Austrian (and Polanyian) account of knowledge as remaining fundamentally "foundational-ist" and rejects the terms of the debate entirely. On his (self-admittedly revisionist) account of Wittgenstein, Pleasants sees the potential productive powers as being entirely outside the scope of scientific inquiry: "Just as the existence of God is not an hypothesis in need of empirical testing, so the possibility and desirability of social-ism – or the inevitability of capitalism – is not a state of affairs to settle via a philosophical or social-scientific *theory*: 'you can fight, hope and even believe without believing *scientifically*'" (emphasis in original; Pleasants 1997, p. 42). While we cannot offer a fair reply to Pleasants here, suffice it to say that his critique of the Austrians is as much a critique of the market socialists or the new technoso-cialists. On his account, a social-scientific debate about the merits of planning is a category mistake. We obviously do not share this view, and neither do any other socialists with whom we engage. Nonetheless, Pleasant's contribution is worth noting if for no other reason than its originality.

From a public administration and policy perspective, Greenwood (2006) revisits the Otto Neurath's contribution to the original debate. Greenwood agrees that Neurath fails to deal with Mises's challenge: the incommensurability of factor valuations in the absence of monetary calculation should produce massive productivity losses under socialism. Greenwood maintains instead that Neurath's chief contribution lay in the suggestion that such productivity losses might be worth incurring for other reasons. Greenwood (2007a) argues that agent-based modeling (ABM) techniques could be useful aids for central planning. We are deeply skeptical, since it seems as though the outcomes of simulations are baked probabilistically into initial conditions; the usefulness of the model (for planning purposes) would depend on the quality of initial conditions and agent programming, but would not be evaluable ex ante. Of course, we could always be surprised. New work on ABMs is interesting, but thus far has not seemed particularly useful for addressing the question of central planning in a world of dynamic uncertainty and tacit knowledge. (Greenwood 2007a) makes a similar argument: "Hayek's argument ultimately hinges upon the contingent claim that the spatio-temporal dispersion of knowledge is too complex for any computational system to address. There might be grounds for challenging this premise, in view of the recent, rapid developments in compu-tational technology" (Greenwood 2007a, 431).

But again, the whole point is that this has never been a computation problem. The knowledge is not "out there" and difficult to collect, but emergent only with the process itself and outside that context does not exist. Given this contextual nature of our knowledge in the market process, the question is, how do we provide guideposts and feedback to decision-makers in a world of dynamic uncertainty, partly endogenously generated through constant innovation, and where the relevant considerations are embedded in large part on the basis of inarticulate hunches and other kinds of tacit knowledge? Surely computational power can help *individuals* make decisions under these conditions. But the great virtue of the market is that decisions receive rapid, unambiguous feedback on granular margins. This results in not only quick adjustments and adaptations to changing circumstances, but adjustments and adaptations that move in a less erroneous direction than before. Prices guide participants to make quick and correct changes in their plans. No analogous mechanism has been shown to be compatible with central planning. It does not matter how few mistakes a mind makes if it is incapable of recognizing and responding to whatever mistakes it does make.

6 Extending the Argument: Applications of the Theory of Economic Calculation

6.1 An Overview of the Calculation Debate's Impact

The socialist calculation debate was not confined to discussions of comparative economic systems. The century-long debate had various streams of influence, and the debate, in turn, influenced the development of subsequent research programs in economics. In a recent *Journal of Economic Literature* survey, Chenggang Xu (2017, pp. 191–192), states clearly that: "From the perspective of mainstream economics, examining the nature of capitalism by understanding socialism can be traced back to the famous theoretical debates of Oskar Lange, Friedrich Hayek, and Ludwig von Mises. This debate significantly influenced general-equilibrium theory (Lange 1936, 1942), information and incentive theory (Hayek 1935, 1945, 1948), and mechanism-design theory (Hurwicz 1972; Myerson 2008). Without this debate, mainstream economics would not be as we see it today." While we agree with the general thrust, we believe Xu is missing some of the most important streams of creative economic theory that flowed directly from the debate and the contributions of Mises and Hayek.

We would emphasize too the development of mechanism design theory and the development of New Institutionalism in the post-WWII era, with our emphasis on the later literature. Mechanism design theory from its founding to its celebratory essays after the Nobel Prize in 2007 always recognized the inspirational role that the calculation debate played in this line of theoretical research. Leonid Hurwicz, for example, traveled first to Geneva to study with Ludwig von Mises and then to LSE to study with Hayek and Robbins as he sought to formulate an effective response to their challenge. As noted earlier,

Jacob Marschak was an early responder to Mises's challenge, and Tjalling Koopmans also sought to respond to Mises–Hayek's challenge in *Three Essays on the State of Economic Science* (1957). This literature focused originally on the question of the informational efficiency of the price system, and thus the informational requirements to engage in scientific planning of the economy. The question of designing the mechanism for resource allocation to align the incentives of the different actors for the accurate revealing of preferences and resource utilization became primary in the work from Hurwicz to more recent contributions by thinkers such as Jean Tirole. Along the way, major developers of modern economic theory from Ken Arrow to Joseph Stiglitz made contributions in information economics and comparative institutional analysis. This literature is vast and beyond our ability here to give it full due. But suffice it to say, that a sentiment of Stiglitz's from his *Whither Socialism?* captures the attitude of many and that is to ponder "whether the insights of modern economic theory and the utopian ideas of the nineteenth century can be brought closer together?" (1994, p. 277) His hopeful answer is yes. There is an optimism that through the right mechanism, the social ills of capitalism can be effectively addressed by government action and we can avoid the trap of repeating the totalitarian experience of the twentieth century, or falling into the intellectual trap of the Chicago School by insisting that we live in the best of all possible worlds.

6.2 James Buchanan and Public Choice

After WWII, economics was transformed. The Great Depression had destroyed the faith in capitalism for at least a generation of thinkers. Keynesianism had ushered in a "New Economics" to replace the pre-war orthodoxy. This "New Economics" was based on macroeconomics and the central notion of aggregate demand management by an activist government. Edward Chamberlin and Joan Robinson, among others, had also effectively challenged the model of perfect competition, and supposedly demonstrated that an unhampered market economy resulted in inefficiencies. Mathematical models and techniques of statistical analysis became the scientific language of modern economics.

Paul Samuelson led this revolution as his best-selling textbook, *Economics* (1948), would dominate undergraduate teaching for the next two generations of students across the English-speaking world, and his *Foundations of Economic Analysis* (1947) transformed the graduate training of PhD students ever since. Most narratives of the post-WWII clash of economics ideas focus on the macroeconomics debate between the Keynesians (Samuelson, Tobin, Solow) and the Monetarists (Friedman) and then New Classical Economics (Lucas and

Sargent). This is often referred to as the "Monetarist Counter-Revolution." This attention makes sense because this is where the major public policy discourse was directed, and of course, Milton Friedman was a uniquely skilled technical economist as well as public intellectual.

But there was another counter-revolution quietly taking place at the same time with respect to microeconomic analysis that challenged the Samuelsonian hegemony. These counter-revolutionaries impacted the development of positive economics, welfare economics and political economy from 1950 to 2000 that are simply overlooked in the more conventional narrative focused on Friedman and the Chicago School.

At a conference at the University of Miami School of Law in 1979, James Buchanan (2015) was asked to reflect on Hayek's contributions to economic science. Buchanan stressed Hayek's emphasis on relative price economics and his focus on the institutional infrastructure of a society of free and responsible individuals. At the end of this essay, Buchanan states that the different strands of economics that emanated from Hayek's project: public choice (Buchanan-Tullock), property rights (Alchian-Demsetz), law-and-economics (Coase) and entrepreneurial theory of the market process (Mises-Hayek-Kirzner) should be productively viewed as conciliatory research programs in modern political economy, as opposed to a source of conflicting paradigms, in the effort to challenge the hegemony of the Samuelsonian neoclassical synthesis. As a matter of personal history, all these individuals sharpened their analysis in a context where the socialist calculation debate loomed in the background.

James Buchanan often repeated the phrase: to say a situation is hopeless is to say it is ideal. As a believer that hope could be found in constitutional change, Buchanan believed strongly that we were not living in the best of all possible worlds. Change in the structural rules of the game, Buchanan insisted, could produce a better situation. The same players and different rules produce different outcomes. Variation in the outcomes was to be explained by the differential impact of alternative institutional arrangements, not on differences in people. People are people.

In developing his research program from the late 1940s onward, Buchanan rejected the idea of a stable social welfare function that the benevolent social planner could maximize. He insisted that one cannot assume within a democratic polity and unified scale of values, what he termed in relation to his chosen field of study – public finance – as the "fisc." Buchanan also insisted that one could not do public finance without postulating a theory of the state, if for no other reason than that one must decide on the appropriate scale and scope of governmental activity prior to asking how best to pay for those activities in an equitable and efficient manner. Social welfare economics, Buchanan would argue, blurs for our analytical vision of the nature of politics as exchange and a functioning democratic political process as one of compromise and turn-taking. This led Buchanan to resurrect political economy mid twentieth century precisely at the height of the economics profession viewing itself as a technical discipline capable of aiding the task of optimal control in exercising social engineering. Such an institutionally antiseptic approach, Buchanan would argue, was surely nonsensical social science. A refrain he would repeatedly stress from these earlier essays to his Nobel Lecture was that economists must cease the practice of proffering advice as if to a benevolent despot. Buchanan's political economy laid the groundwork for what he called "genuine institutional economics." The task, he argued, was for economists to not be content to take as given the institutional infrastructure within which economic activity takes place, but to derive the institutional framework itself from the ordinary behavioral assumptions from which the economist commences their analysis. In Buchanan's scientific development, this focus on institutions and the theory of the state evolved into public choice analysis and constitutional political economy.

Buchanan also harbored an interest in the calculation debate directly. This is seen in his discussion of the debate in *Cost and Choice* ([1969] 1999), as well as several other essays that contrasted his understanding of the spontaneous order of the market with the effort to engage in what he sometimes called "managerial socialism." Buchanan recognized that a "modern reading of these early contributions by Mises [on the problem of economic calculation] suggests that some of the intuitive force of his argument stemmed from a more sophisticated conception of opportunity cost than he was able to make explicit at that time" (Buchanan [1969] 1999, p. 21). For Mises (and later Hayek), opportunity costs are not objective constraints to which individuals passively respond, as conceptualized by the neoclassical market socialists in their understanding of "parametric" pricing under socialism. Rather, opportunity costs are subjective variables of choice that only emerge as a by-product of exchange.

6.3 Ronald Coase and the New Institutionalists

Ronald Coase, while a student at the LSE in the 1930s, was led to pursue his transaction-cost approach due to a puzzle that first occurred to him in Arnold Plant's lecture on the socialist calculation debate (Coase 1992, p. 715). He sought to understand why if economic planning was rife with problems, commercial activities weren't organized in spot markets exclusively. On the other hand, if planning could work at the individual firm level, why not at the industry level, or the national level, or the international level? Coase's proposed answer was the concept of transaction costs, and these costs are all those costs associated with engaging in acts of exchange and production. Spot markets are workable, but costly, so firms arise to minimize transaction costs. On the other hand, firms must meter and monitor the performance of their employees, and as those costs rise, they will turn to markets to provide the necessary goods and services. Entrepreneurial alertness and creativity are exhibited throughout the process, as market opportunities are created, recognized, and seized upon. Coase in pursuing his transaction cost analysis was able to study the organization of economic activity in firms, the impact of alternative legal rules on economic performance, and the operation of markets across various settings.

Coase's theory of the firm (1937) should be understood as fundamentally contributing to the calculation debate. Planning is itself an activity that must be subject to economic calculation. The amount of central planning to be undertaken has costs and benefits. Firms allocate by fiat internally to economize on transaction costs; they trade in spot markets where transaction costs are sufficiently low. One way (the Austrian way) of reading Coase (1937) is this: there is a nonzero optimal level of ignorance about asset values. Allocating resources by fiat within a firm prevents them from being subject to market exchanges, and thus, from being priced. The conclusion of the calculation argument is that resources cannot be rationally allocated if no capital good is ever priced. Which raises the question: how much can we reasonably leave unpriced?

The answer latent in Coase (1937) is made explicit by Piano and Rouanet (2020) who argue that the boundaries of the firm are determined by a kind of *economic calculation*. In deciding whether to make or buy, firms assess the benefits of spot markets (clear market valuations of capital) relative to the (transactions) costs of using such markets. But importantly, they make these decisions within the broader context of a marketplace and thus receive feedback in the form of profit and loss on whether they correctly evaluate make-or-buy decisions. Seen in these terms, the error of the socialists should be still more obvious. The socialist view maintains that the optimal number of firms is unity. But the optimal size and number of firms are ambiguous and need to be discovered by the marketplace. More importantly, however, Coase's fundamental point goes beyond drawing the boundaries between markets and firms, but the role that institutions play in facilitating the process of economic calculation. Drawing an implicit connection back to the Austrians, Coase states, "a large part of what we think of as economic activity is designed to accomplish what high transaction costs would otherwise prevent or to reduce transaction costs so that individuals can freely negotiate and we can take advantage of that diffused knowledge of which Hayek has told us" (1992, p. 716).

It is worth noting further that some earlier Austrians drew an explicit connection to Coase. Rothbard (1962) and Klein (1996) make the argument that the problem of economic calculation will prevent small firms from agglomerating into one enormous firm in the limit. They draw on Coase to show that firm size is determined by transaction costs. Transaction costs are the marginal costs of using the market to engage in economic calculation (Boettke et al. 2023). They unite this insight with the Austrian tradition by pointing out that economic calculation is the marginal benefit of using the market. The more one transacts in spot markets, and the less he allocates by fiat, the more calculable are the values of his assets and capital, and the more measurable their marginal contributions to his output. Metering and monitoring can take place within the organization *via* the price system. Firms thus expand to the point where the marginal benefit of expansion equals the marginal cost – and no further. As long as there is some point at which calculation is more valuable than transaction costs are costly, there will exist a multitude of firms, and they will not integrate into a single entity.

6.4 Armen Alchian, Harold Demsetz, and UCLA Price Theory

Armen Alchian and Harold Demsetz are two other major economists impacted by the Mises–Hayek position in the socialist calculation debate. Alchian is often considered in the folklore of the profession as an economist's economist. How his mind worked and why it so impressed his peers is illustrated perfectly by an episode from his time at the Rand Corporation in the 1950s as the Cold War was ramping up. Both the US and Soviet nuclear programs were cloaked in secrecy. As the development of the hydrogen bomb was classified information, Alchian suggested that one could track the critical resources in the production process by studying publicly available financial data. And by following the price movements, Alchian was able to identify lithium as the fissile fuel that was being utilized. It was the use of lithium that enabled the development of high-yield nuclear weapons deliverable by aircraft. Alchian's study was immediately confiscated and destroyed as a "threat to national security."[19] But, his brilliance as an analyst utilizing the economic way of thinking to cut through complicated and confusing matters to find a straightforward solution was solidified.

This isn't the only example one could give of Alchian's mind unearthing the *economic forces at work* in everyday life. He wrote fundamental papers in economic theory and applied economics, but he is perhaps best known for his book with William Allen, *University Economics*, which was first published in 1964 and sought to communicate the power of basic economic reasoning and, in

---

[19] For a discussion of this episode see Newhard (2014).

particular, basic price theory to college students. The book became a classic reference for faculty and graduate students who resisted the dominant macroeconomic approach of the time. And, it served as the introduction to economics to generations of college students. It was the first textbook to challenge the hegemony of Paul Samuelson's *Economics*, reassert the primacy of microeconomic analysis, and provide microfoundations for discussing monetary analysis and policy. Samuelson's text, it must be remembered, did not introduce supply and demand analysis, let alone individual choice discussions, until well after the full treatment of macroeconomic concepts such as National Income Accounting and the tools of aggregate demand management. Only when the macroeconomic system was in balance, Samuelson taught, could the microeconomic analysis of supply and demand and the examination of the market economy at the industry, and even firm, level take place. Alchian and Allen effectively reversed that order in *University Economics* and built the analysis from the individual to the firm to the industry to the economic system.

The intellectual foundations of Alchian's work can be traced back to Mises and Hayek in several ways. In the UCLA oral history interviews (Hayek [1978] 1983), Alchian explains while interviewing Hayek how as a student in the 1930s two books would shape his life work.[20] This comes after a rather charming moment when Alchian quizzes Hayek on the meaning of price changes in the context of inflation. When Hayek gives the "right" answer focusing on *relative prices* as guides to exchange and production decisions, Alchian smiles and informs Hayek that he got the answer right. In the interview, Alchian also discusses how as a student he read Hayek's *Prices and Production* (1931), which led to his own emphasis on relative prices as guides in his explanation of exchange and production, and how reading Berle and Means's *The Modern Corporation and Private Property* (1932) challenged him to provide an answer to the problem of the separation of ownership from control in terms of the organization of firms and their governance. *Property, prices, and profit-and-loss* have been the focus of Alchian's economic analysis ever since. In short, Alchian's positive impression of Hayek's analysis in *Prices and Production* sharpened his negative impression of the argument in Berle and Mean's *The Modern Corporation and Private Property* and set the agenda for his subsequent career in the development of what became known as the property rights paradigm.

Consider two of Alchian's most famous papers: "Uncertainty, Evolution and Economic Theory" (1950) and "Some Economics of Property Rights" (1965).

---

[20] Alchian was, in fact, set to move to London to pursue his PhD at the LSE under the direction of Hayek and Robbins, but the outbreak of WWII changed those plans.

These illustrate the fruits of his learning not only from Hayek, but also from his reading of Mises. As recollected by Henry Manne, one of the intellectual founders of law and economics and a close colleague of Alchian's,[21] he has stated that Alchian (1950) *"is very much in the tradition of market process economics, not Chicago equilibrium stuff"* (emphasis added; quoted in Zywicki 2014, p. 547, fn. 6). Alchian (1950) is generally read in terms of what Mark Blaug (1980) refers to as the "Alchian Thesis," the notion, presumably originated by Alchian himself, that firms act *as if* they are profit-maximizing. Not only is the claim absolutely false, but importantly, this Chicago-style interpretation of Alchian's argument regarding firm behavior undermines its explanatory power. In a world of uncertainty, Alchian argues that profit maximization, *understood in perfectly competitive terms*, is a meaningless standard by which to evaluate firm behavior (Alchian 1950, p. 211). Alchian is very clear that in "an economic system the realization of profits is the criterion according to which successful and surviving firms are selected" (1950, p. 213). "Realized positive profits, not *maximum* profits, are the mark of success and viability" (emphasis original; 1950, p. 213). He goes further to argue that the "crucial element is one's aggregate position relative to actual competitors, not some hypothetically perfect competitors ... *Even in a world of stupid men there would still be profits"* (1950, emphasis added). Therefore, contrary to the traditional interpretation of the Alchian Thesis, "[t]here are no implications of "profit maximization," and this difference is important" (Alchian 1950, p. 217), because "[t]he pursuit of profits, and not some hypothetical undefinable perfect situation, is the relevant objective whose *fulfilment* is rewarded with survival" (Alchian 1950, p. 218). None of this implies that firm owners are unpurposive or irrational, but it does imply that the postulate of profit-maximization is neither a necessary nor a sufficient condition for understanding firm behavior. Individuals will be led to that decision by the economic forces *at work* within the market context. If, for a variety of reasons, individuals are not confronted with the competitive pressure of substitutes and the discipline of hard-budget constraints, then of course the economic forces *at work* in that situation will steer their behavior in a different direction in predictable ways.

Alchian's "Some Economics of Property Rights" (1965), according to Manne, "was stimulated by his reading Mises's *Human Action"* (quoted in Zywicki 2014, p. 547, fn. 6), as Manne also recounts and further elaborates in an oral interview to the Securities and Exchange Commission Historical Society (see Manne 2012). Human action, Alchian explained, follows the basic logic of

---

[21] Beginning in 1976 at the University of Miami Law & Economics Center, Henry Manne developed and directed educational programs in economics for federal judges, for which Alchian had been hired by Manne as one of the principal instructors (see Butler 1999).

economics that private property rights concentrate the rewards-costs more directly on the individual decision-maker, while public ownership disperses those rewards-costs more widely. This has consequences – neither good nor bad by definition, but also not trivial. The property rights structure in operation changes the methods and manner in which objectives will be pursued. As Alchian says, he is just following Adam Smith when he writes that individuals will "redirect their activities as they seek to increase their utility or level of satisfaction of their desires" when there are "changes in the rewards-costs structure" (1965, p. 822). Whereas most of the economics literature talks about the division of labor in society, Alchian wanted to get fellow economists to think about the division of ownership in society. Under a private property ownership structure, there will emerge a pattern of resource ownership that is tailored to unique skills and talents. People differ, Alchian stresses, "in their talents as owners." They have different abilities to bear risk, to make decisions about what to make, how much to make, the best method to make it, how much to invest in the enterprise, and who shall be employed in the processes of production and distribution as laborers and as managers. "Ownership ability," he concludes, "includes attitude toward risk bearing, knowledge of different people's productive abilities, foresight, and, of course, 'judgment'" (Alchian 1965, p. 825). And, this ownership structure is put to the test every day in the private property market economy. Less so, in the public ownership regime of government activity. There the test is different, the rewards-costs structure is different, and thus the behavior is different. Again, just as Adam Smith taught.

Alchian (1965, p. 825, emphasis added) further adds: "If ownership rights are transferable, *then specialization of ownership will yield gains.* People will concentrate their ownership in those areas in which they believe they have a comparative advantage if they want to increase their wealth. Just as specialization in typing, music, or various types of labor is more productive *so is specialization in ownership.* Some people specialize in electronics industry knowledge, some in airlines, some in dairies, some in retailing, etc. *Private property owners can specialize in knowledge* about electronics, devoting much of their effort and study to learning which electronic devices show promise, which are now most efficient in various uses, which should be produced in larger numbers, where investment should take place, what kinds of research and development to finance, etc." Like Hayek before him, Alchian stressed that the division of labor entails a division of knowledge in society.[22] However, in developing the argument, he also demonstrated that both

---

[22] As Hayek (emphasis original, 1937, p. 49) puts it, "Clearly there is here a problem of the *Division of Knowledge* which is quite analogous to, and at least as important as, the problem of the division of labour."

a division of labor and a division of knowledge (or mental division of labor as Mises puts it) are by-products of a division of ownership, illustrating that Mises and Hayek's contributions to the socialist calculation debate are flip sides of the same coin.

So, why did Alchian have to recapture such a basic point of common knowledge in economics from Adam Smith onward? The institutional framework, which was so critical to the classical political economists, went from being treated as given to being forgotten. And with that, any hope of critical analysis of the impact of alternative institutional arrangements on the pursuit of productive specialization and peaceful social cooperation through exchange was lost in the professional literature. The increasing distance between the mainstream literature in 1950–1975 from the earlier presentations of the competitive market process and the liberal political and legal structure within which the economy was embedded is an indicator of just how far economic theory had become derailed by the desire to have an institutionally antiseptic science of economics.

Alchian and Demsetz (1972) wrote a seminal text on the theory of the firm from a property rights perspective. Demsetz (1964, 1967) also published several key papers on the economics of property rights related to the origin, operation, and consequences of the assignments of rights in economic activity. Demsetz (1968, 1973) also wrote some of the key papers discussing the implications of market rivalry for public policy. Many of these contributions mirror arguments one reads in Mises and Hayek. In his article "The Exchange and Enforcement of Property Rights," Demsetz makes the point about economic calculation and the knowledge problem as follows: "This valuation function is related to but distinct from the incentives to work provided by a property system, for even in a society where work is viewed as a pleasurable activity, and, hence, where incentives to work are not needed, it would still be necessary to properly value the varieties of alternative output that can be produced" (1964, p. 18).

Buchanan, Coase, Alchian, and Demsetz all agitated in the post-WWII period to bring institutions back into economic analysis. Once this aspect of the evolution of modern economics is recognized, then Hayek's works during the 1950–1980 period, such as *The Constitution of Liberty* (1960) and *Law, Legislation and Liberty* (1973, 1976, 1979) take on a new significance. Rather than being viewed as abandonments of economics, which his peers often did, the reality is he was drawing his readers' attention to the institutional infrastructure within which economic activity is played out. Hayek was simply the first New Institutional Economist. But this was not understood at the time. To the extent it came to be understood was in no small measure due to the pioneering effort of Armen Alchian, James Buchanan, Ronald Coase, Harold Demsetz, and Gordon Tullock.

6.5 Israel Kirzner and the Entrepreneurial Market Process

Israel Kirzner's (1988) development of the entrepreneurial theory of the market process also followed from his reading of the socialist calculation debate. It was in that debate, that the program of Mises and Hayek to study the market *process* as opposed to market *equilibrium* is articulated with clarity, and with that the nonparametric function of relative prices. As Hayek stressed, prices are not summaries of past activity, but guides to future decisions. Treating prices as sufficient solutions to an equilibrium puzzle missed out on their functional significance in the coordination of economic activity and the power of the price system. However, by the 1950s this equilibrium paradigm had taken such root that economists, such as Nobel laureates Kenneth Arrow and Gerard Debreu (as well as Frank Hahn), became preoccupied with proving the existence, stability, and uniqueness of competitive equilibrium in markets as "a reasonably accurate description of reality" (Arrow and Debreu 1954, p. 265). So ingrained was such equilibrium theorizing that in a paper ironically titled "Toward a Theory of Price Adjustment," Arrow argued the following:

> Under conditions of disequilibrium, there is no reason that there should be a single market price, and we may very well expect that each firm will charge a different price ... The law that there is only one price on a competitive market (Jevons's Law of Indifference) is derived on the basis of profit- or utility-maximizing behavior on the part of both sides of the market; but there is no reason for such behavior to lead to unique price except in equilibrium, or possibly under conditions of perfect knowledge. (Arrow 1959, p. 46)

Given this intellectual context, the evolution of Kirzner's scholarship can be understood as a consistent explication of the entrepreneurial role in the market process. One way in which to situate the importance of Kirzner's seminal contributions is in terms stated by his student, Don Lavoie (1991, p. 39): "Mainstream economics, according to Kirzner, is not so much wrong as simply incomplete." Rather than a pre-reconciliation of plans required in the Walrasian system, the Kirznerian rendering of the price system focuses on the role of the entrepreneur in the reconciliation of economic plans among producers and consumers. As Kirzner puts it in his *Market Theory and the Price System* (emphasis original, 1963, p. 222): "If a market is not in equilibrium, we have seen, this must be the result of ignorance by market participants of relevant market information. The market process, as always, performs its functions by impressing upon those making decisions those essential items of knowledge that are sufficient to guide them to make decisions *as if* they possessed the complete knowledge of the underlying facts."

Relative prices guide us in our decision-making, profits lure us in our decisions, and losses discipline us in our decisions. This is how the price system impresses upon us the essential items of knowledge required for plan coordination. Or, as he would summarize the point in his *JEL* essay "Entrepreneurial Discovery and the Competitive Market Process": "The entrepreneurial process so set into motion, is a process tending toward better mutual awareness among market participants. The lure of pure profit in this way sets up the process through which pure profit tends to be competed away. Enhanced mutual awareness, via the entrepreneurial discovery process, is the source of the market's equilibrative properties" (Kirzner 1997, p. 72).

It was these critical lessons that were learned in the socialist calculation debate that focused analytical attention on the institutional framework and the processes in operation that enable the coordination of economic activity through time. The production plans of some must mesh with the consumption demands of others, and they must mesh in a way that both strives to eliminate waste at any point in time and be capable of constant adaptation and adjustment to changing circumstances through time. Rational economic calculation within a private property commercial society is able to do this – this is the mechanism by which the "invisible hand" is achieved. It is not some social alchemy that transforms self-interest into the public interest, as critics sometimes accuse the classical and early neoclassical economists of postulating. Rather, the governing dynamics of the invisible hand of the market rely on the role of relative prices in guiding, the lure of profit, the discipline of loss, and overall the security of persons and property that structures incentives so that the entire social learning process can get initiated in the first place.[23] Positive political economy must study property rights, prices, profit-and-loss, and the political infrastructure within which economic activity takes place if we are to make progress in understanding how alternative institutional arrangements impact the ability of individuals to pursue productive specialization and realize peaceful social cooperation in a manner that produces the miracle of modern economic growth.

7 Conclusion

Perhaps the most telling success of the Austrian argument is the role that the calculation debate played in shaping the counter-revolution in microeconomics in the second half of the twentieth century. Moreover, the calculation debate

---

[23] This is why Boettke (2018) summarizes Hayek's contribution as one of developing an *epistemic institutionalism* perspective of economics and social processes.

represents one of the most significant clashes of economic ideas in the history of our science. This debate taught us that institutions matter, that knowledge is contextual, that markets exhibit adaptative efficiency, and that methods and methodologies that cloud our understanding of the functional significance of monetary economic calculation to the operation of the economic system must be resisted. Ironically, as Hayek stressed in various writings in the sciences of complex phenomena, of which economics is a prime example, it is often the case that approaches that appear the most scientific are often the least helpful for advancing the science, and those that appear least scientific often turn out to be the most helpful. We point the reader back to Boulding's remarks on the scientific fruitfulness of the "literary borderland between economics and sociology" in contrast to the barrenness of the "flawless precision of mathematical economics." This debate highlights this point perhaps more than any other in the history of economic thought.

The insights developed and refined during the debate carried implications for questions far outside the argument's original scope. Contemporary rejoinders to the Austrian position have improved on older socialist arguments in important ways yet continue to miss the essential point we have argued. We live in a world of scarcity, which implies that we must always be negotiating trade-offs. We want to produce more with less, not less with more. And it doesn't matter whether what we are producing is to serve our highest ideals of justice, or to satisfy our basest materialistic desires. We cannot afford to have systematic waste. But in order to negotiate these trade-offs we require tools to aid the human mind. Within a commercial society, those tools come in the form of property, prices, and profit-and-loss. The constellation of the price system enables individuals in the system to have reliable indicators to aid in assessing the trade-offs in exchange and production decisions. The market process is based on the ability to engage in rational economic calculation. What economic calculation does is enable the social system of exchange and production to sort from the array of technologically feasible projects those that are economically viable. In this way the desirable is checked by the feasible and the feasible in turn is checked by the viable. Systemic waste is eliminated. Note we didn't just say waste, but systemic waste, because there will always be errors and failed projects that need recalculation. The power of the market is not limited to its ruthless efficiency, but to its constant adaptation and adjustment set in motion by recognition of opportunities for entrepreneurial profit through arbitrage and/or innovation. This is how the system produces more with less, rather than less with more. It is how the economic system copes with the implications of scarcity.

We live in a dynamic and changing world, and in such a world what this debate has taught us is that the dispersed and tacit nature of knowledge means that attempts at central planning must remain a fatal conceit. In the end, the unrefuted Austrian argument is a call to humility. Economics as a discipline has given us powerful insights about the world, but it has not given us anything approaching mastery of the world. We economists practice the worldly philosophy and seek to understand the world around us by offering us answers to questions of existing phenomena of *what* happened and when; of *why* what happened happened; and *how* it all works to come about. These are questions of fact, of function, and of operation. Economics makes sense of the seemingly senseless. The properly trained economist, with the aid of the basic principles of economic reasoning, can rise to the height of an observational genius, while a genius without the tools of economic reasoning at their disposal is often reduced to confusing noise with sense. Economics provides a tool for social understanding. What it doesn't do is provide a tool of social control.

That conclusion matters because the twentieth century was dominated by the effort to achieve social control, and economics was transformed in that effort to meet that task. It failed miserably. And it led to the sterile economics that had to be discarded in the counter-revolution of property rights, law and economics, public choice and market process economics. The rediscovery of a genuine institutional economics that has its roots in the classical political economists but is informed by the developments in economic theory attributed to the early neoclassical economists should have been enough to temper the enthusiasm for economics as a tool for social engineering. At first, it did, and then it didn't.

Our hope is that our Element has contributed to learning the lessons that this century-long debate among economists has taught us about the nature and significance of economic theory. The fact that socialism seems to be in the midst of a revival means that the call to humility to economists is as relevant today as it was when Mises first put forward his original challenge in 1920 and 1922. It also means that the essential contributions of this debate have yet to be fully incorporated into the mainstream of economic thought and teaching. There is still much work to do in that regard.

References

Adaman, F., & Devine, P. (1996). The economics calculation debate: Lessons for socialists. *Cambridge Journal of Economics*, **20**(5), 523–537.

Adaman, F., & Devine, P. (2022). Revisiting the calculation debate: A call for a multiscale approach. *Rethinking Marxism*, **34**(2), 162–192.

Alchian, A. A. (1950). Uncertainty, evolution, and economic theory. *Journal of Political Economy*, **58**(3), 211–221.

Alchian, A. A. (1965). Some economics of property Rights. *Il Politico*, **30**(4), 816–829.

Alchian, A. A., & Allen, W. R. (1964). *University Economics: Elements of Inquiry*, 1st edition. Belmont: Wadsworth.

Alchian, A. A., & Demsetz, H. (1972). Production, information costs, and economic organization. *The American Economic Review*, **62**(5), 777–795.

Anderson, G. M., & Boettke, P. J. (1997). Soviet venality: A rent-seeking model of the communist state. *Public Choice*, **93**(1/2), 37–53.

Armentano, D. (1969). Resource allocation problems under socialism. In W. P. Snavely, ed., *Theory of Economic Systems: Capitalism, Socialism, and Corporatism*. Columbus: Charles E. Merrill, pp. 127–139.

Arnold, N. S. (1987a). Marx and disequilibrium in market socialist relations of production. *Economics and Philosophy*, **3**(1), 23–47.

Arnold, N. S. (1987b). Final reply to Professor Schweickart. *Economics and Philosophy*, **3**(2), 335–338.

Arnold, N. S. (1987c). Further thoughts on the degeneration of market socialism: A reply to Schweickart. *Economics and Philosophy*, **3**(2), 320–330.

Arrow, K. J. (1959). Toward a theory of price adjustment. In *The Allocation of Resources: Essays in Honor of Bernard Francis Haley*. Stanford: Stanford University Press, pp. 41–51.

Arrow, K. J., & Debreu, G. (1954). Existence of an equilibrium for a competitive economy. *Econometrica*, **22**(3), 265–290.

Arthur, W. B. (2023). Economics in nouns and verbs. *Journal of Economic Behavior & Organization*, **205**, 638–647.

Bardhan, P., & Roemer, J. E. (1992). Market socialism: A case for rejuvenation. *Journal of Economic Perspectives*, **6**(3), 101–116.

Baumol, W. J. (2002). Entrepreneurship, innovation and growth: The David-Goliath symbiosis. *The Journal of Entrepreneurial Finance and Business Ventures*, **7**(2), 1–10.

Bergson, Abram. (1948). Socialist economics. In H. Willis, ed., *A Survey of Contemporary Economics*. Philadelphia: Blakiston, pp. 412–448.

Berle, A. A., & Means, G. C. (1932). *The Modern Corporation and Private Property*. London: Macmillan.

Blaug, M. (1980). *The Methodology of Economics: Or How Economists Explain*. New York: Cambridge University Press.

Bockman, J., Fischer, A., & Woodruff, D. (2016). "Socialist accounting" by Karl Polanyi: with preface "socialism and the embedded economy." *Theory and Society*, **45**(5), 385–427.

Boettke, P. J. (1990). *The Political Economy of Soviet Socialism: The Formative Years, 1918–1928*. Dordrecht: Kluwer.

Boettke, P. J. (1993). *Why Perestroika Failed: The Politics and Economics of Socialist Transformation*. London: Routledge.

Boettke, P. J. (1995). Why are there no Austrian socialists? Ideology, science and the Austrian school. *Journal of the History of Economic Thought*, **17**(1), 35–56.

Boettke, P. J. (2005). On reading Hayek: Choice, consequences and *The Road to Serfdom*. *European Journal of Political Economy*, **21**(4), 1042–1053.

Boettke, P. J. (2018). *F. A. Hayek: Economics, Political Economy and Social Phiolosophy*. London: Palgrave Macmillan.

Boettke, P. J., & Candela, R. A. (2015). What is old should be new again: Methodological individualism, institutional analysis and spontaneous order. *Sociologia*, **2**, 5–14.

Boettke, P. J., & Candela, R. A. (2017). The intellectual context of F. A. Hayek's *The Road to Serfdom*. *Journal of Private Enterprise*, **32**(1), 29–44.

Boettke, P. J., & Candela, R. A. (2019). Liberalism in crisis and the promise of a reconstructed liberalism. *Journal of Contextual Economics – Schmollers Jahrbuch*, **139**(2–4), 189–212.

Boettke, P. J., & Candela, R. A. (2020). The Austrian school of economics: A view from London. *The Review of Austrian Economics*, **33**(1–2), 69–85.

Boettke, P. J., & Candela, R. A. (2023). On the feasibility of technosocialism. *Journal of Economic Behavior and Organization*, **205**, 44–54.

Boettke, P. J., Candela, R. A., & Jacobsen, P. (2023). Economic calculation and transaction costs: The case of the airline oversales auction system. *Southern Economic Journal*, **89**(3), 708–731.

Böhm-Bawerk, E. v. ([1896] 1898). *Karl Marx and the Close of His System*, translated by Alice M. Macdonald. New York: Macmillan.

Böhm-Bawerk, E. v. ([1884] 1959). *Capital and Interest, Volume I: History and Critique of Interest Theories*, translated by George D. Huncke and Hans Sennholz. Spring Mills: Libertarian Press.

Böhm-Bawerk, E. v. ([1889] 1959). *Capital and Interest, Volume II: Positive Theory of Capital*, translated by George D. Huncke and Hans Sennholz. Spring Mills: Libertarian Press.

Böhm-Bawerk, E. v. ([1921] 1959). *Capital and Interest, Volume III: Further Essays on Capital and Interest*, translated by George D. Huncke and Hans Sennholz. Spring Mills: Libertarian Press.

Boettke, P. J., & Leeson, P. T. (2002). Hayek, Arrow, and the problems of democratic decision-making. *The Journal of Public Finance and Public Choice*, **20**(1), 9–21.

Boulding, K. E. (1948). Samuelson's *Foundations*: The role of mathematics in economics. *Journal of Political Economy*, **56**(3), 187–199.

Buchanan, J. M. ([1969] 1999). *The Collected Works of James M. Buchanan, Volume 6, Cost and Choice: An Inquiry in Economic Theory*. Indianapolis: Liberty Fund.

Buchanan, J. M. (2015). Notes on Hayek – Miami, 15 February, 1979. *The Review of Austrian Economics*, **28**(3), 257–260.

Buchanan, J. M., & Tullock, G. (1962). *The Calculus of Consent: Logical Foundations of Constitutional Democracy*. Ann Arbor: University of Michigan Press.

Bukharin, N. (1927). *The Economic Theory of the Leisure Class*. London: Martin Lawrence.

Burczak, T. A. (2006). *Socialism after Hayek*. Ann Arbor: University of Michigan Press.

Butler, H. N. (1999). The Manne programs in economics for federal judges. *Case Western Reserve Law Review*, **50**(2), 351–420.

Caldwell, B. (1997). Hayek and socialism. *Journal of Economic Literature*, **35**(4), 1856–1890.

Caldwell, B. (2007). Introduction. In B. Caldwell, ed., *The Road to Serfdom: Text and Documents*. Chicago: University of Chicago Press, pp. 1–35.

Caldwell, B. (2020). *The Road to Serfdom* after 75 Years. *Journal of Economic Literature*, **58**(3), 720–748.

Coase, R. H. (1937). The nature of the firm. *Economica*, **4**(16), 386–405.

Coase, R. H. (1992). The institutional structure of production. *The American Economic Review*, **82**(4), 713–719.

Cockshott, W. P. (1990). Application of artificial intelligence techniques to economic planning. *Future Computer Systems*, **2**(4), 429–443.

Cockshott, W. P., & Cottrell, A. (1993). *Towards a New Socialism*. Nottingham: Spokesman.

Cottrell, A., & Cockshott, W. P. (1993). Calculation, complexity and planning: The socialist calculation debate once again. *Review of Political Economy*, **5** (1), 73–112.

Dekker, E. (2016). *The Viennese Students of Civilization: The Meaning and Context of Austrian Economics Reconsidered.* Cambridge: Cambridge University Press.

Demsetz, H. (1964). The exchange and enforcement of property rights. *The Journal of Law & Economics*, **7**, 11–26.

Demsetz, H. (1967). Toward a theory of property rights. *American Economic Review*, **57**(2), 347–359.

Demsetz, H. (1968). Why regulate utilities? *Journal of Law & Economics*, **11** (1), 55–65.

Demsetz, H. (1973). Industry structure, market rivalry, and public policy. *Journal of Law & Economics*, **16**(1), 1–9.

Dickinson, H. D. (1933). Price formation in a socialist community. *The Economic Journal*, **43**(170), 237–250.

Durbin, E. (1985). *New Jerusalems: The Labor Party and the Economics of Democratic Socialism.* London: Routledge.

Durbin, E. F. M. (1945). Professor Hayek on economic planning and political liberty. *The Economic Journal*, **55**(220), 357–370.

Ebeling, R. M., ed. (2000). *Selected Writings of Ludwig von Mises, Volume 3: The Political Economy of International Reform and Reconstruction.* Indianapolis: Liberty Fund.

Ebeling, R. M., ed. (2002). *Selected Writings of Ludwig von Mises, Volume 2: Between the Two World Wars: Monetary Disorder, Interventionism, Socialism, and the Great Depression.* Indianapolis: Liberty Fund.

Ebeling, R. M., ed. (2012). *Selecting Writings of Ludwig von Mises, Volume 1: Monetary and Economic Policy Problems Before, During, and After the Great War.* Indianapolis: Liberty Fund.

Farrant, A., & McPhail, E. (2010). No good deed goes unpunished? Revisiting the Hayek-Samuelson exchange over Hayek's alleged "inevitability" thesis. *History of Economic Ideas*, **18**(3), 87–103.

Fisher, F. M. (1983). *Disequilibrium Foundations of Equilibrium Economics.* New York: Cambridge University Press.

Foley, D. K. (2020a). Socialist alternatives to capitalism I: Marx to Hayek. *Review of Evolutionary Political Economy*, **1**(3), 297–311.

Foley, D. K. (2020b). Socialist alternatives to capitalism II: Vienna to Santa Fe. *Review of Evolutionary Political Economy*, **1**(3), 313–328.

Friedman, M. (1947). Lerner on the economics of control. *Journal of Political Economy*, **55**(5), 405–416.

Greenwood, D. (2006). Commensurability and beyond: From Mises and Neurath to the future of the socialist calculation debate. *Economy and Society*, **35**(1), 65–90.

Greenwood, D. (2007a). Planning and know-how: The relationship between knowledge and calculation in Hayek's case for markets. *Review of Political Economy*, **19**(3), 419–434.

Greenwood, D. (2007b). From market to non-market: An autonomous agent approach to central planning. *The Knowledge Engineering Review*, **22**(4), 349–360.

Harper, D. (1996). *Entrepreneurship and the Market Process: An Enquiry into the Growth of Knowledge*. New York: Routledge.

Hayek, F. A. (1931). *Prices and Production*. London: Routledge.

Hayek, F. A. (1933). The trend of economic thinking. *Economica*, **40**, 121–137.

Hayek, F. A., ed. (1935). *Collectivist Economic Planning*. London: Routledge & Kegan Paul.

Hayek, F. A. (1937). Economics and knowledge. *Economica*, **4**(13), 33–54.

Hayek, F. A. (1938 [2012]). *Freedom and the Economic System*. Mansfield Centre: Martino.

Hayek, F. A. (1940). Socialist calculation: The competitive "solution." *Economica*, **7**(26), 125–149.

Hayek, F. A. ([1944] 2007). *The Road to Serfdom*. Chicago: University of Chicago Press.

Hayek, F. A. (1945). The use of knowledge in society. *American Economic Review*, **30**(4), 519–530.

Hayek, F. A. (1948). *Individualism and Economic Order*. Chicago: University of Chicago Press.

Hayek, F. A. (1952). *The Counter-Revolution of Science: Studies on the Abuse of Reason*. Glencoe: The Free Press.

Hayek, F. A. (1960). *The Constitution of Liberty*. Chicago: University of Chicago Press.

Hayek, F. A. (1973). *Law, Legislation and Liberty, Volume 1: Rules and Order*. Chicago: University of Chicago Press.

Hayek, F. A. (1976). *Law, Legislation and Liberty, Volume 2: The Mirage of Social Justice*. Chicago: University of Chicago Press.

Hayek, F. A. ([1978] 1983). *Nobel Prize-Winning Economist: Friedrich A. von Hayek*. Los Angeles: The Regents of the University of California.

Hayek, F. A. (1979). *Law, Legislation and Liberty, Volume 3: The Political Order of a Free People*. Chicago: University of Chicago Press.

Hayek, F. A. (1982). Two pages of fiction: The impossibility of socialist calculation. *Economic Affairs*, **2**(3), 135–142.

Hayek, F. A. (1988). *The Fatal Conceit: The Errors of Socialism*. Chicago: University of Chicago Press.

Hayek, F. A. (2018). *The Collected Works of F.A. Hayek, Volume 13: Studies on the Abuse and Decline of Reason*, edited by Bruce Caldwell. Indianapolis: Liberty Fund.

Heilbroner, R. (1990). Reflections after communism. *The New Yorker*, September 10, **60**(30): 91–100.

Hilferding, R. ([1910] 1981). *Finance Capital*. London: Routledge.

Hodgson, G. M. (2018). *Wrong Turnings: How the Left Got Lost*. Chicago: The University of Chicago Press.

Hodgson, G. M. (2019). *Is Socialism Feasible? Towards an Alternative Future*. Northampton: Edward Elgar.

Hodgson, G. M. (2021). *Liberal Solidarity: The Political Economy of Social Democratic Liberalism*. Northampton: Edward Elgar.

Hoff, T. J. B. ([1938] 1949). *Economic Calculation in the Socialist Society*. London: William Hodge.

Hurwicz, L. (1969). On the concept and possibility of informational decentralization. *American Economic Review*, **59**(2), 513–524.

Hurwicz, L. (1972). On informationally decentralized systems. In C. B. McGuire, & R. Radner, eds., *Decision and Organization: A Volume in Honor of Jacob Marschak*. Amsterdam: North Holland, pp. 297–336.

Keynes, J. M. ([1926] 1978). The end of laissez-faire. In E. Johnson, & D. Mogridge, eds., *The Collected Writings of John Maynard Keynes, Volume IX: Essays in Persuasion*. New York: Cambridge University Press, pp. 272–294.

King, B., & Petty, R. (2021). *The Rise of Technosocialism: How Inequality, AI and Climate Will Usher in a New World*. Singapore: Marshall Cavendish International.

Kirzner, I. M. (1963). *Market Theory and the Price System*. Princeton: D. Van Nostrand.

Kirzner, I. M. (1973). *Competition and Entrepreneurship*. Chicago: University of Chicago Press.

Kirzner, I. M. (1988). The economic calculation debate: Lessons for Austrians. *The Review of Austrian Economics*, **2**(1), 1–18.

Kirzner, I. M. (1992). *The Meaning of Market Process: Essays in the Development of Modern Austrian Economics*. London: Routledge.

Kirzner, I. M. (1997). Entrepreneurial discovery and the competitive market process: An Austrian approach. *Journal of Economic Literature*, **35**(1), 60–85.

Klein, P. G. (1996). Economic calculation and the limits of organization. *Review of Austrian Economics*, **9**(2), 3–28.

Knight, F. H. (1936). The place of marginal economics in a collectivist system. *American Economic Review*, **26**(1), 255–266.

Koopmans, T. (1957). *Three Essays on the State of Economic Science.* New York: McGraw Hill.

Kripke, S. A. (1982). *Wittgenstein on Rules and Private Language: An Elementary Exposition.* Cambridge, MA: Harvard University Press.

Lachmann, L. M. (1977). *Capital, Expectations, and the Market Process: Essays on the Theory of the Market Economy.* Kansas City: Sheed Andrews and McMeel.

Lange, O. (1936). On the economic theory of socialism: Part one. *The Review of Economic Studies*, **4**(1), 53–71.

Lange, O. (1937). On the economic theory of socialism: Part two. *The Review of Economic Studies*, **4**(2), 123–142.

Lange, O. (1967). The computer and the market. In C. H. Feinstein, ed., *Socialism, Capitalism & Economic Growth: Essays Presented to Maurice Dobb.* New York: Cambridge University Press, pp. 158–161.

Laski, H. (1942). *A Planned Economic Democracy: The Labour Party Report of the 41st Annual Conference.* London: Transport House.

Lavoie, D. (1985a). *Rivalry and Central Planning: The Socialist Calculation Debate Reconsidered.* New York: Cambridge University Press.

Lavoie, D. (1985b). *National Economic Planning: What Is Left?* Cambridge: Ballinger.

Lavoie, D. (1986). The market as a procedure for discovery and conveyance of inarticulate knowledge. *Comparative Economic Studies*, **28**, 1–19.

Lavoie, D. (1991). The discovery and interpretation of profit opportunities: Culture and the Kirznerian entrepreneur. In B. Berger, ed., *The Culture of Entrepreneurship.* San Francisco: Institute for Contemporary Studies, pp. 33–51.

Lerner, A. P. (1934). Economic theory and socialist economy. *The Review of Economic Studies*, **2**(1), 51–61.

Lerner, A. P. (1935). Economic theory and socialist economy: A rejoinder. *The Review of Economic Studies*, **2**(2), 152–154.

Lerner, A. P. (1936). A note on socialist economics. *The Review of Economic Studies*, **4**(1), 72–76.

Lerner, A. P. (1944). *The Economics of Control.* New York: Macmillan.

Levy, D. M. (1990). The bias in centrally planned prices. *Public Choice*, **67**(3), 213–226.

Levy, D. M., & Peart, S. J. (2011). Soviet growth and American textbooks: An endogenous past. *Journal of Economic Behavior & Organization*, **78**(1–2), 110–125.

Lippmann, W. (1937). *The Good Society.* Boston: Little, Brown.

Lopes, T. C. (2021). Technical or political: The socialist economic calcluation debate. *Cambridge Journal of Economics*, **45**(4), 787–810.

Manne, H. (2012). Interview with Henry Manne conducted on August 6, 2012 by James Stocker. *Securities and Exchange Commission Historical Society.* www.sechistorical.org/collection/oral-histories/20120806_Manne_Henry_T.pdf.

Marx, K. ([1932] 1988). *Economic and Philosophic Manuscripts of 1844.* Amherst: Prometheus Books.

Marx, K., & Engels, F. ([1846] 1939). *The German Ideology.* New York: International.

Mark, K., & Engels, F. ([1848] 1998). *The Communist Manifesto.* New York: Signet Classic.

McCloskey, D. N. (2006). *The Bourgeois Virtues: Ethics for an Age of Commerce.* Chicago: University Of Chicago Press.

McCloskey, D. N. (2019). *Why Liberalism Works How True Liberal Values Produce a Freer, More Equal, Prosperous World for All.* New Haven: Yale University Press.

Mill, J. S. Mill. ([1848] 1965). *Collected Works of John Stuart Mill, Volume II: Principles of Political Economy with Some of Their Applications to Social Philosophy.* Toronto: University of Toronto Press.

Mises, L. v. ([1912] 1981). *The Theory of Money and Credit.* Indianapolis: Liberty Fund.

Mises, L. v. ([1919] 2006). *Nation, State, and Economy: Contributions to the Politics and History of Our Time.* Indianapolis: Liberty Fund.

Mises, L. v. (1920). Die wirtschaftsrechnung im sozialistischen gemeinwesen. *Archiv für Sozialwisssenschaft Sozialpolitik*, **47**, 86–121.

Mises, L. v. ([1920] 1975). Economic calculation in the socialist commonwealth. In F. A. Hayek, ed., *Collectivist Economic Planning.* Clifton: Augustus M. Kelly, pp. 87–130.

Mises, L. v. ([1922] 1981). *Socialism: An Economic and Sociological Analysis.* Indianapolis: Liberty Fund.

Mises, L. v. ([1927] 2005). *Liberalism: The Classical Tradition.* Indianapolis: Liberty Fund.

Mises, L. v. ([1949] 1966). *Human Action: A Treatise on Economics*, 3rd ed. Chicago: Henry Regnery.

Mises, L. v. (1957). *Theory and History.* New Haven: Yale University Press.

Mises, L. v. (1960). *Epistemological Problems of Economics.* Princeton: D. Van Nostrand.

Morozov, E. (2019). Digital socialism: The calculation debate in the age of big data. *New Left Review*, **116/117**, 33–67.

Myerson, R. B. (2008). Perspectives on mechanism design in economic theory. *American Economic Review*, **98**(3), 586–603.

Nelson, R. R., & Winter, S. G. (1982). *An Evolutionary Theory of Economic Change*. Cambridge, MA: Harvard University Press.

Newhard, J. M. (2014). The stock market speaks: How Dr. Alchian learned how to build the bomb. *Journal of Corporate Finance*, **27**, 116–132.

Nutter, G. W. (1968). Markets without property: A grand illusion. In N. A. Beadles, & L. A. Drewry, Jr., eds., *Money, the Market, and the State: Essays in Honor of James Muir Waller*. Athens: University of Georgia Press, pp. 137–145.

Peart, S. J., & Levy, D. M. (2009). After Hayek: On Theodore Burczak's socialism after Hayek. *The Review of Austrian Economics*, **22**(3), 293–296.

Penrose, E. T. (1959). *The Theory of the Growth of the Firm*. Oxford: Blackwell.

Piano, E. E., & Rouanet, R. (2020). Economic calculation and the organization of markets. *The Review of Austrian Economics*, **33**(3), 331–348.

Pigou, A. C. (1944). *The Road to Serfdom* by F. A. Hayek. *The Economic Journal*, **54**(214), 217–219.

Piketty, T. (2021). *Time for Socialism: Dispatches from a World on Fire, 2016–2021*. New Haven: Yale University Press.

Pleasants, N. (1997). The epistemological argument against socialism: A Wittgensteinian critique of Hayek and Giddens. *Inquiry: An Interdisciplinary Journal of Philosophy*, **40**(1), 23–45.

Polanyi, M. (1951). *The Logic of Liberty*. Chicago: University of Chicago Press.

Polanyi, M. (1958). *Personal Knowledge: Towards a Post-Critical Philosophy*. Chicago: University of Chicago Press.

Polanyi, M. (1966). *The Tacit Dimension*. Garden City: Double Day.

Prychitko, D. L. (1991). *Marxism and Workers' Self-Management: The Essential Tension*. New York: Greenwood Press.

Prychitko, D. L. (2002). *Markets, Planning and Democracy: Essays after the Collapse of Communism*. Northampton: Edward Elgar.

Robbins, L. (1952). *The Theory of Economic Policy in English Classical Political Economy*. London: Macmillan.

Rothbard, M. N. (1962). *Man, Economy, and State: A Treatise on Economic Principles*. Princeton: D. Van Nostrand.

Samothrakis, S. (2021). Artificial intelligence inspired methods for the allocation of common goods and services. *PLoS ONE*, **16**(9), e0257399.

Samuelson, P. A. (1947). *Foundations of Economic Analysis*. Cambridge, MA: Harvard University Press.

Samuelson, P. A. (1948). *Economics*. New York: McGraw-Hill.

Samuelson, P. A., & Nordhaus, W. D. (1989). *Economics*, 13th ed. New York: McGraw-Hill.

Say, J. B. ([1803] 1964). *A Treatise on Political Economy*. New York: Augustus M. Kelly.

Schumpeter, J. A. (1942). *Capitalism, Socialism, and Democracy*. New York: Harper & Brothers.

Schweickart, D. (1987a). Market socialist capitalist roaders: A comment on Arnold. *Economics & Philosophy*, **3**(2), 308–319.

Schweickart, D. (1987b). A reply to Arnold's reply. *Economics & Philosophy*, **3** (2), 331–334.

Shapiro, D. (1989). Reviving the socialist calculation debate: A defense of Hayek against Lange. *Social Philosophy & Policy*, **6**(2), 139–159.

Shleifer, A., & Vishny, R. W. (1992). Pervasive shortages under socialism. *The RAND Journal of Economics*, **23**(2), 237–246.

Shleifer, A., & Vishny, R. W. (1994). The politics of market socialism. *The Journal of Economic Perspectives*, **8**(2), 165–176.

Smith, A. ([1776] 1976). *An Inquiry into the Nature and Causes of the Wealth of Nations*. Chicago: University of Chicago Press.

Stiglitz, J. E. (1994). *Whither Socialism?* Cambridge, MA: MIT Press.

Taylor, F. M. (1929). The guidance of production in a socialist state. *American Economic Review*, **19**(1), 1–8.

Truitt, T., & Burns, S. (forthcoming). Economic calculation and the role of prices in privatization. *The Independent Review: A Journal of Political Economy*.

Vaughn, K. I. (1980). Economic calculation under socialism: The Austrian contribution. *Economic Inquiry*, **18**(4), 535–554.

Vaughn, K. I. (1994). *Austrian Economics in America*. New York: Cambridge University Press.

Wasserman, J. (2019). *The Marginal Revolutionaries: How Austrian Economists Fought the War of Ideas*. New Haven: Yale University Press.

Weber, M. ([1918] 1967). *Socialism*, translated with an introduciton by H. F. Dickie-Clark (Occasional Paper No.11). Durban: Institute for Social Research.

Weber, M. ([1921] 2013). *Economy and Society*. Berkeley: University of California Press.

Wieser, F. (1893). *Natural Value*. London: Macmillan.

Xu, C. (2017). Capitalism and socialism: A review of Kornai's *Dynamism, Rivalry, and the Surplus Economy*. *Journal of Economic Literature*, **55**(1), 191–208.

Zywicki, T. J. (2014). Keynote address: Is there a George Mason school of law and economics? *Journal of Law, Economics & Policy*, **10**(3), 543–554.

Acknowledgments

We wish to acknowledge Christopher Coyne and Caleb Fuller, whose close reading, feedback, and comments greatly improved the drafting of this manuscript. A very special thanks are also due to Jessica Carges for her editorial comments. We are also grateful for the intellectual support provided by the F.A. Hayek Program at the Mercatus Center, George Mason University. Rosolino Candela also expresses a particular debt of gratitude for the support provided by Angus Burgin and the Center for Economy and Society at Johns Hopkins University, where this manuscript was completed during his time as a Visiting Fellow. Any remaining errors are entirely our own.

Cambridge Elements ⹀

Austrian Economics

Peter Boettke

George Mason University

Peter Boettke is a Professor of Economics & Philosophy at George Mason University, the BB&T Professor for the Study of Capitalism, and the director of the F. A. Hayek Program for Advanced Study in Philosophy, Politics and Economics at the Mercatus Center at George Mason University.

About the Series

This series will primarily be focused on contemporary developments in the Austrian School of Economics and its relevance to the methodological and analytical debates at the frontier of social science and humanities research, and the continuing relevance of the Austrian School of Economics for the practical affairs of public policy throughout the world.

Cambridge Elements ≡

Austrian Economics

Elements in the Series

A full series listing is available at: www.cambridge.org/EAEC

Printed in the United States
by Baker & Taylor Publisher Services